MW01282060

1st John

Living in Christ: Bible Study/Commentary Series

Steve Copland

1st John
Living in Christ: Bible Study/Commentary Series
Published by Steve Copland at Createspace
Copyright 2018 by Steve Copland

Steve Copland is a self-supported missionary/Pastor from New Zealand, serving The Lord in Ukraine since 2003. He is a former lecturer at the Ukraine Evangelical Seminary and International Christian University.

Table of Contents

1st John

Introduction

It is becoming increasingly obvious that we are living in those times when, as Paul prophesied, 'men will not put up with sound doctrine' (2nd Timothy 4:3). Charismatics predict a great revival ushered in by an army of miracle workers, whilst the Scriptures speak of a great apostasy. Added to this are two other extremes among more conservative denominations. The new Calvinists continue to teach that God has predestined the masses to hell, despite verses which teach that the Lord 'wants all men to be saved and come to a knowledge of the truth' (1st Timothy 2:4), and they insist that God's sovereignty wipes out any place for human decision or responsibility, even in the final call to surrender all to Christ.

Evangelicals, on the other hand, have placed such an extreme on human decision that God's sovereignty is diminished to a point where He seems to be sitting on His throne and forced to hand out the gift of the Holy Spirit to anyone, of any age, who 'asks Jesus into his heart'. The modern gospel is devoid of any hint of carrying our cross, counting the cost, or forsaking the world, so we have unregenerate churchgoers living in fornication, practicing homosexuals in leadership roles, and people running around claiming they were 'born again' as young as four years old, as if a child even had a life of their own to give to Christ.

Although some of this false theology is relatively new, the problem of unregenerate people claiming to be

Christians is not. This letter of John's is a case in point. By the time this letter was written, at least 35 years after the Church began at Pentecost, apostasy, false doctrines and teachers were rife. In this letter John gives us twelve specific marks by which to identify a true Christian. Many of them concern evidence of a changed life, whilst others reveal false teachings. All of these are given, not to point fingers at others, but rather to examine ourselves.

Authorship

This first letter of John's is somewhat different in that it does not state the name of the author, nor is it addressed to anyone in particular, as is customary for a letter. Although it identifies its readers as 'dear children' (2:1, 5:21) it is more like a written sermon than the traditional format of a 1st century letter. Even though the author never gives his name, scholars recognize the similarities in style and context to the Gospel of John, the apostle who walked with Jesus. For example, no other writer uses the title of Word (logos) for Jesus other than John, and this writing style is very similar to the opening of John's gospel.

Date

Scholars differ in dating the letter. It may have been written before John's gospel, which is considered to be in the latter part of the 1st century, but like the gospel there is no reference to major events such as the fall of Jerusalem in AD 69-70, or persecutions under the reign of the Emperor Nero which began in AD 64, therefore, some suggest that it was written prior to these events. The book of Revelation, also penned by John, seems to have very strong references to Nero's reign, so perhaps there is a good case to suggest that, had these persecutions started at the time of writing this letter, John would have made reference to the effects they were having on the Church.

Whilst the case for a timeline before AD 64 has merits, it is also possible that the fall of Jerusalem was such a well-known event that it needed no mention in any of the apostle's letters. Scholars, who point to a date beyond AD 64, point to John's well developed Christology, which is prevalent throughout his writings. This is clearly seen in this particular letter which is written to combat Docetism, which itself emerged from the Gnostics. With all of these factors in mind, it would seem most unlikely that the letter is earlier than the mid seventies, and possibly even a decade later.

Reasons for Writing

The system which became known as Gnosticism was well established by the middle of the second century, a system of belief which, according to Irenaeus in his *Against Heresies*, can been traced back to the teachings of Simon the Sorcerer of Acts 8. This system emphasized a form of secret knowledge (*gnosis*) which was known only to a select few, and often said to be received through the mediation of angels. Knowledge is a key issue in this letter of John's, in fact he uses the Greek verbs 'to know' (*ginosko*) twenty-five times and (*oida*) fifteen times. The apostle Paul confronted early forms of this system in his letters to the Colossians and Corinthians, and in this writing of John's we see the author confronting another developing Gnostic belief, namely, Docetism.

Docetism comes from the word *'doce'* which means 'to appear'. The Docetists, like those later referred to generally as Gnostics, claimed that all of the material world was inherently evil. Although the later system of Gnosticism claimed that Jehovah was a jealous and evil God, and this teaching was certainly started during the lifetime of Simon Magus, many of the early Docetists still considered God (Jehovah) to be good and, therefore, unable to be associated with matter in any way. It is important to understand that Magus (and the Gnostics) taught that the Supreme God was Sophia, not Jehovah, and that Jesus Christ was created directly by Sophia. Therefore, both groups denied that God could be incarnate in the person of Jesus Christ and that Jesus only *seemed* to have a body of flesh, he only 'appeared' to be human.

It is doubtful that John is confronting full-blown Docetism as he never uses words such as 'phantom' which appear in later Gnostic writings, however, the theme of Christ's real bodily incarnation occurs throughout, therefore, my view is that John recognizes and is anticipating the Gnostic teachings which seriously attacked true Christian doctrine and spawned some 40 false gospels. (For more on Gnostic teachings see *Religion: History and Mystery* on www.stevecopland.com).

John understands that the heresy of Docetism attacks the very foundations of Christianity, and without truth, there can be no real and abiding fellowship, either with God or those who know God. Therefore, he gives the following reason for his letter:

3 We proclaim to you what we have seen and heard, so that you also may have fellowship with us. And our fellowship is with the Father and his Son, Jesus Christ. 4 We write this to make our joy complete.

This letter, as we shall refer to it, shares some very practical advice and challenges to Christians regarding the issues of sin, and fellowship, both with God and other members of the Body of Christ, which we will study as we work through the chapters. One of the most powerful themes throughout the letter is love. John challenges us about what and who we love; God, our brothers and sisters, or are we still in love with the world?

Another fundamental theme of the letter is in what I have termed 'marks' of a true Christian, which we will identify in each study. John often uses phrases which challenge his readers to examine whether or not they really know, love and obey Christ. He also speaks of the 'anointing', the indwelling presence of the Holy Spirit which must be present within all who claim to be Christian, the same Spirit which testifies to the non-negotiable truths he declares regarding the nature of Jesus Christ, His Divinity and humanity.

To Whom

As previously mentioned, there are several fatherly terms of care used in the letter which indicate the writer's concern for those he considered his spiritual children, such as 'dear children', 'little children let no one deceive you' etc. In both 2nd and 3rd John, the writer refers to himself as 'The Elder' a term used to indicate both apostolic authority, and the heart of an overseer to shepherd those in his care.

Study One

Prologue 1st John 1:1-4

1 That which was from the beginning, which we have heard, which we have seen with our eyes, which we have looked at and our hands have touched - this we proclaim concerning the Word of life. 2 The life appeared; we have seen it and testify to it, and we proclaim to you the eternal life, which was with the Father and has appeared to us.

3 We proclaim to you what we have seen and heard, so that you also may have fellowship with us. And our fellowship is with the Father and his Son, Jesus Christ. 4 We write this to make our joy complete.

In these first four verses John confronts the heresy of Docetism head on. In his introductory sentences John begins with two non-negotiable doctrines of the Christian faith, namely, that Jesus Christ is both God and man.

That which was from the beginning. These words echo the first verses of Genesis and are continued in his title for Christ as the 'Word of Life' which we will discuss shortly. John takes us back to the beginning of creation to introduce us to the fact of the incarnation; that the One who was there in the beginning has appeared as a man (John 1:14).

John uses the Greek *'phaneroo'*, which the NIV has translated as 'appeared', an unusual translation choice considering the fact that the author is writing to refute the Docetists claim that Christ was a mere apparition. As discussed in the introduction, the word *'doce'* means to appear or to *seem* to be real, but John has intentionally used a word which means to be manifested, to be a real physical entity. His use of *'phaneroo'* is a direct contradiction to the Docetists teaching that Jesus only appeared to be a real person.

Notice too how often he hammers home his point with the phrases *we have seen with our eyes, looked at* and *our hands have touched.* These phrases are telling his readers that Christ was a real man, not a phantom. He tells us that the Word of Life was manifested, we have seen and testify to His physical reality. The *we* are the apostles who walked with Jesus, ate with Him, saw Him, touched Him, and He is and was the Eternal Life manifest in the flesh.

If any man could testify about the true Divine and human natures of Jesus Christ it was John. John lived with Jesus for three years. He knew the man he'd shared countless meals with, the man he travelled with, sleeping under the stars. He saw the Jesus who grew tired after speaking to the crowds and healing their sick for hours, the man who went into the hills alone to pray, and the Jesus who wept as He stood before the tomb of His friend Lazarus. No doubt there are countless conversations he'd had with Jesus which are not mentioned in his gospel, but those events he wrote about obviously amazed him.

He was there that day, early in the Lord's ministry, when Jesus performed hundreds of miracles, fed a crowd of around 20,000 people (including women and children), sent the disciples away in a boat, and then came to them walking on the water (Matthew 14). That night John and the others thought they were seeing a phantom, crying out in terror, "it's a ghost", for Jesus was glowing with the majesty of God, much the same as He did on the Mount of Transfiguration, an experience John shared with Peter and James (Matthew 17:1-8, Luke 9: 28-36, 2nd Peter 1:16-18).

And no doubt he was there when Jesus appeared to His disciples after He resurrected. Jesus realized that some of them thought He was a ghost and invited them to touch Him, to see that He had real flesh and bones (Luke 24:38-39). On that occasion the risen Christ asked for food and ate fish in front of them all, and a short time later He cooked them breakfast on the beach by the Sea of Galilee (John 21:12).

John lived with Jesus for three years and had no doubts about His humanity and Divinity. He had many moments when he was challenged to make decisions about the nature of Jesus, as would any who witnessed the things he saw, and therefore, he has unrivaled authority to make the claims he does in his introductory sentences of this letter.

What did John believe about Jesus' Divinity?

John says He was *there in the beginning* and calls Him the *Word of Life*, a reference to Christ as the *Logos* (Word) and Creator which, either echo the first verses of his gospel - if we consider it was written first - or are a precursor to the Christology of the gospel. The gospel of John opens with the words:

1. In the beginning was the Word, and the Word was with God and the Word was God. 2 He was with God in the beginning. 3 Through him all things were made;

without him nothing was made that has been made (John 1:1-3).

14 The Word became flesh and dwelt for a while among us. We have seen His glory, the glory of the one and only Son, who came from the Father, full of grace and truth (John 1:14).

Jesus Christ is the Logos, He is God the Son who became the Son of God and lived for a time among us. He is the Creator of all that exists and the One who reveals the Godhead to us (Colossians 2:9). This same Logos became 'flesh' (John1:14). The word flesh is the Greek *sarx,* a word used throughout the New Testament (NT) to describe our physical bodies and human nature. We will discuss the implications of *sarx,* as it applies to Jesus, in study six.

John also tells us twice in his prologue that he and the apostles of Christ proclaim this message of the incarnation; they, like him, are witnesses to the physical reality of Jesus, and all proclaim the same message, so that those who hear and believe may have fellowship together with the apostles, and fellowship with the Father and Jesus Christ.

Why does John consider the heresy of Docetism such a serious issue?

1. Firstly, if Jesus Christ was a mere phantom there has been no real sacrifice offered for sin, and therefore, there is no salvation in Him. God's holy wrath against sin demands a real, physical sacrifice in order for perfect justice to be fulfilled. This fact is taught throughout the Old Testament and witnessed in the animal sacrifices

conducted by the Levitical priesthood. Sin brought death (Romans 5:12), and only blood, which is the symbol of life, can cancel the debt of sin. Jesus' sacrifice was real, a life given to redeem us from death, His blood had to be shed in order to fulfill the debt owed to the Father on our behalf. If He was a mere phantom, then no debt has been paid, it was all a deception, indeed, Docetism was in essence claiming that God was a cheat.

2. Secondly, we must take note of John's use of the word *fellowship*, which we will discuss deeply in our next two studies. This is the Greek *koinonia* which means to possess something in common. For Christians, this means the binding of one to another through the fact that we possess the Holy Spirit, and also, that we are God's own possession (Ephesians 1:14). John understands that those who have been filled with the Holy Spirit know that Jesus Christ is both God the Son, the 'Word', and the real manifestation as the Son of God.

He reminds his readers later that they have an anointing from the Holy Spirit and *all of them know the truth* (1st John 2:20). True Christian fellowship can only occur through the common indwelling of the Holy Spirit, and no true Christian can believe that Christ was a phantom if the Spirit dwells within them, for it is He who reveals this truth.

3. Thirdly, John is saying that there is no real fellowship with those who deny the full humanity and Divinity of Christ. It is not a matter of agreeing to disagree, it is a matter of eternal life or eternal damnation. The humanity and Divinity of Christ are non-negotiable. If Jesus was not 100% human He could never be our substitute for sin, and if He is not 100% Divine He cannot save, for only God can save.

In His humanity He reaches down to where we are, taking upon Himself human nature with all its weaknesses, and in His Divinity He lifts us up to the very throne room of God where He is Savior, Redeemer and Judge. It is a delusion to believe that Christians can have fellowship with those such as Mormons and Jehovah's Witnesses who deny the full humanity or Divinity of Jesus Christ, and it is equally deluded to suggest that such have received the gift of the Holy Spirit.

Summary

Within the Christian faith there are non-negotiable truths which are its very foundation. The Incarnation is the most fundamental of these truths, a truth which was foretold throughout the Old Testament and fulfilled in the birth, life, death and resurrection of Jesus Christ. The human mind cannot comprehend what Paul calls the 'mystery of God' (Colossians 2:3), for we cannot understand how our Creator could become a part of His own creation. For this reason many cults have arisen for the past two thousand years, beginning with Docetism and Gnosticism (and later Arianism), denying either the full humanity or Divinity of Jesus Christ.

There is no salvation for people who insist on remaining in such ignorance, for in essence they demand that God submit His plans to their pathetic intellects, indeed, they defiantly refuse to believe what cannot be fully understood. But there is something far more powerful than mere intellectual understanding which can only be experienced by those who choose to believe, namely, conviction. Conviction occurs when the Holy

Spirit testifies with our spirit the truth of the nature of Jesus Christ. It is difficult to explain to those who have never experienced it, because it is the very voice of God Himself witnessing to our spirit. It is this witness of the Spirit (Romans 8:16-17) that testifies that we are God's children, and without it, there can be no true fellowship either between 'believers', or a person and God.

Throughout this letter John identifies several marks or proofs which may be used to determine whether or not a person is a true believer. These are given, not as a formal judgment, but rather as tests for individuals to examine themselves to see that they are really in the faith.

Study Two

The First Mark: Fellowship with God

1st John 1:5-6

5 This is the message we have heard from him and declare to you: God is light; and in him is no darkness at all. 6 If we claim to have fellowship with him yet walk in the darkness, we lie and do not walk by the truth. 7 But if we walk in the light, as he is in the light, we have fellowship with one another, and the blood of Jesus, his Son, purifies us from all sin.

In our first study I wrote that there can be no true fellowship with those who deny the full humanity and Divinity of Jesus Christ: this truth is one of the marks of a true Christian. The reason for this is simple in that it is the indwelling Spirit of God who reveals these truths to us at the time of our conversion. When we are born again we become, as Peter writes, *partakers of the Divine nature* (2nd Peter 1:4). The word 'partakers', that Peter uses, comes from the same root as John's use of *koinonia* which is translated 'fellowship'. To have fellowship is to have something in common. After salvation we have the Divine nature in common with our holy Creator, and with all of our brothers and sisters in Christ. See how John describes the Divine nature.

God is light; and in Him there is no darkness at all.

This statement declares the infinite holiness of God which can never compromise with sin. This is the moral perfection of the Divine Nature, that which Christians have received and desire to imitate. John is about to speak about sin in our lives, so he reminds us of the nature of God, a nature that we have received, and then challenges us as to whether or not His nature is being manifest in our lives.

In verse 5 John tells us of the message he has heard, that *God is light and in him there is no darkness at all*. It is likely that he has heard this message from Jesus Himself, for Christ is the subject of the previous verse, yet nowhere in the gospels do we find Jesus using these exact words. We know that Jesus frequently referred to Himself as the Light of the World and the Light that came into the world, and also claimed that He and the Father are one, therefore, John may be simply declaring the indivisibility of God and Christ, for there is no doubt that John considered Jesus to be God, the Word, the Creator (John 1:1) who came from the Father (John 1:14).

However, in this particular case, it is likely that he is primarily referring to the invisible Father, for he makes a distinction in verse 7, writing, *the blood of Jesus, his Son, purifies us from all sin*. The apostle may also be underlining the real humanity of Jesus in this verse with his reference to the *blood of Jesus*.

In especially his gospel, John frequently records the claims of Jesus Christ as the Light which dispels the darkness (John 1:4-5, 7-9, 3:19-21, 8:12, 9:5, 12:35-36, 46). This was a common theme of Jesus and one that John takes up here in his first letter. Whenever light enters a dark place those things which were hidden become visible, even those which lurk in the shadows. John is about to challenge his readers about knowing Christ, and he will tell us later in this letter that *whosoever claims to live in him must walk as Jesus walked* (2:6).

His point is simple to understand! Jesus had perfect fellowship with the Father during His life on earth because He continually walked in the light. If we claim to have this same fellowship, then we must walk accordingly, therefore, John tells us in verse 6 *that if we claim to have fellowship with him, yet walk in the darkness, we lie and do not live by the truth.*

Here, then, is the first of John's marks of a true Christian.

If we claim to have fellowship with God then we are claiming to be born again (John 3:3), to be new creations (2nd Corinthians 5:17) and partakers of the Divine nature (2nd Peter 1:4). This means that Christ, the light of men, is living within us, and we are hidden in Him (Colossians 3:3). Remember that the word *koinonia* (fellowship) means to have something in common, therefore, if we do not share the Divine nature in common with God we have no real fellowship with Him.

How then can we be sure that we have this fellowship?

John gives us practical advice, and a way to test ourselves, using the analogies of light and darkness. The light of Christ initially exposes the desires of our sinful natures, those things which belong to the world of darkness. We refer to this as the conviction of the Holy Spirit (John 16:9). It is this conviction which calls us to repent and trust in Christ as Lord and Savior. As we surrender ourselves to Christ we are born again and the Divine nature takes up residence within us (John 14:18, 23). From this moment onwards we begin to walk in the light for the light Himself has taken up residence within us and guides our steps into new life (Romans 6:5).

How, John asks, can one who has the light of Christ continue to walk in darkness?

To walk in darkness is to live in ignorance of the truth of ourselves as sinners; it is to live without regard to the moral excellence of the Divine Nature, and to walk devoid of fellowship with our holy Creator. No person who is united with Christ can continue to walk in such darkness, for this would be a complete contradiction to the power and miracle of new birth. If a person claims to be born of God, yet does not walk as Jesus walked (2:6), this person deceives themselves. In other words, if there is no evidence of a changed and changing life, then we should seriously doubt that new birth has occurred.

There are some who teach that anyone who makes a declaration of Jesus as their Savior is automatically born again, whether or not they produce fruits which accompany salvation. Such people claim to have led hundreds to Christ, most of whom they never see again. I have had several debates with self-proclaimed evangelists who enjoy posting their exploits on social media regarding their 'soul-winning' activities. One particular person approaches strangers with the introduction, 'do you realize that Jesus loves you?'. He then proceeds to explain that this person is a sinner, but all he needs to do is to ask God's forgiveness for sinning and believe that Jesus has saved him from God's wrath. The person then repeats a simple prayer and 'receives Jesus into their heart'. After writing of these experiences on social media there is often the words, 'I hope this new-born comes to church'.

However much I may applaud the intentions of such evangelists, I am dismayed at the lack of understanding regarding what is required for a person to be born again. This topic is discussed in-depth in the first chapter of *Running the Race,* which is available as a free download on my website (www.stevecopland.com), and is beyond the scope of this study.

However, Scripture is replete with warnings about evidence of a changed life such as the verses we are studying here. Jesus' parable of the sower and the seed (Matthew 13) is a good example of recognizing that not all who appear to begin the Christian life will continue in it to the evidence of producing spiritual fruit. Jesus' analogy of Himself as the vine (John 15) confirms that, unless we are producing the fruits of the Spirit, we are not in Christ.

New birth is much more than an intellectual consent to Christian teachings, indeed, it is the beginning of a new life of walking in the light through the illumination and power of the Divine Nature dwelling within us. To walk in the light is to live in step with the desires of our new nature, a desire for holiness, for sanctification, set apart to live in God's will. These are the desires which accompany the presence of Christ within us, and if they are absent, we cannot claim to have fellowship with God.

For the new-born in Christ, we should never have to wonder, 'I hope they come to church', for the Holy Spirit brings with His presence a hunger for fellowship, a hunger to know God's Word and a hunger to live in the light that we have received. The apostle Peter uses this exact analogy when describing new Christians. He writes;

Like newborn babies, crave pure spiritual milk, so that by it you may grow up in your salvation, now that you have tasted that the Lord is good (1st Peter 2:2-3).

Summary

Fellowship with God is fundamental to new birth! Fellowship is to share something in common, and in this case, to share in the very nature of God as partakers of His Divine nature (2nd Peter 1:3-4). When we have been spiritually united with Christ we naturally begin to share Jesus' desire to walk in complete obedience to the Father, as Jesus did whilst upon this earth. As we walk in the light we have received, we begin to produce the fruit of the Holy Spirit who dwells within us. We are in the Vine, and His nature and power flow into us, producing fruit which accompanies regeneration, new birth.

This is the first of John's marks of a true Christian, the evidence of a changed and changing life, one that loves to walk in the light, illuminated by the glory of God, for *God is light: in him is no darkness at all.* This does not mean that we will never stumble, but rather, because of the Divine nature within us, we *make every effort to add to our faith goodness; and to goodness, knowledge; and to knowledge, self-control; and to self-control, perseverance; and to perseverance, godliness; and to godliness, brotherly kindness; and to brotherly kindness, love (2nd Peter 1:5-7).*

Study Three

Fellowship with Believers

1st John 1:3,7

3 We proclaim to you what we have seen and heard, so that you also may have fellowship with us. And our fellowship is with the Father and his Son, Jesus Christ.

7 But if we walk in the light, as he is in the light, we have fellowship with one another, and the blood of Jesus, his Son, purifies us from all sin.

In this study we will examine what *koinonia* (fellowship) means in terms of relationships within the Body of Christ.

In our previous study we saw that every true Christian has received the Divine nature and shares this nature in common with God. The sharing of His nature is the foundation of our fellowship with Him, and the reason Scripture states that we belong to Him. Romans 8:9 tells us that when we have the Spirit of Christ we belong to Christ. Likewise, Ephesians 1:13-14 says that the Holy Spirit within us guarantees our inheritance in Christ and that we are 'God's possession'.

In this letter of John's, the apostle brings this into a family context and calls us *children of God (1st John 3:1-2)*. All of these passages speak initially of our new relationship with God, but in turn they also lay the foundation of our relationships with fellow Christians in what Scripture describes as the Body of Christ.

So what does it really mean that we are parts of the Body of Christ and children of God?

Like me, you've probably heard many sermons about the Body of Christ in respect of spiritual gifts; we are asked, are we a hand, a foot, a mouth etc? Spiritual gifts are one very important aspect of the Body of Christ, but another, of equal importance is too often neglected, namely, that we *belong to each other*.

In Romans 12:5 Paul tells us that *in Christ we who are many form one body, and each member belongs to all the others.* Although Paul is writing here in the context of spiritual gifts, he is also addressing another problem within the Church at Rome, namely, divisions within the Body of Christ. Likewise, in 1st Corinthians 12:12-27 Paul stresses the fact of us belonging to *one body* (v12), that every part of that body is essential (v13-24), that we *should have equal concern for each other* (v25), *and that if one part suffers, every other part suffers with it; if one part is honored, every part rejoices with it* (v26).

As children of God we have been adopted into one spiritual family, and Scripture has a great deal to say about what that means in terms of our relationships with one another.

Unfortunately, much of what the early Church practiced as *koinonia* has been all but lost in our emphasis on individualism in Western cultures. We tend to think of family as one thing, and Church as another. We may sometimes use the term 'Church family', but do we really see other members of the Body of Christ in the same way as we view our natural blood-relatives? If we compare what John understands as 'fellowship', and our modern Church practices, we may be challenged in many areas.

Individualism

There is no doubt that the Scriptures call individuals to respond to the gospel and be saved. During the spread of Roman Catholicism during the Middle Ages, this doctrine was all but abandoned. Popes, even 'evangelical' popes such as Gregory of the seventh century, ordered priests to convert Kings and Queens who then declared their entire realms to be 'Christian'. In general terms, the biblical concept of individual salvation only appears rarely during this period until the Protestant Reformation. In Scripture there *are* examples of entire households being saved at the same time (Acts 10), yet never the idea that anyone was considered to be Christian without an individual response.

However, from the moment of regeneration individuals become part of something far greater than themselves, namely, the Body of Christ. Within this Body each person is a vital part of the whole (1st Corinthians 12;12-26), and in general terms will give an account of their individual lives to the Lord in respect to how they lived and served within the Body (Romans 14:12). Yet today many professing Christians believe that they need not be subject to any other member of the Body of Christ, and view their Bible as their sole authority.

Imagine a Church with no Bibles or Church buildings. Today, Western Christians usually own several copies of the Bible and in different translations, but the early Church had almost nothing in terms of written Scripture. Those who met in synagogues may have had access to Old Testament scrolls, but in the main people met in each other's homes.

Within about 30 years from the Day of Pentecost, a few copies of the apostles' letters may have begun to circulate, but until this time Christians had to rely upon each other. The Body of Christ provided the inspired teaching until the written Word became available. One member would speak in tongues (a language unlearned) and two others would interpret the message given. They had to rely upon each other even to receive a 'sermon' within their meetings.

Today, many Western Christians rely on their own interpretation of Scripture and spend hours arguing over which translation is the best, and on social media heated debates and individualism, rather than unity, are the norm. Those 'friends' on Facebook who agree with every detail of one's interpretation are considered 'brothers and sisters', and the others are 'unfriended' as heretics. This attitude extends beyond the internet. Such people forsake any real *koinonia*, leave various congregations and live in isolation from other Christians.

In the other extreme there is the 'mega Church' trend, many of which promote a celebrity leader who is a law unto himself and subject to no one, a trend which is equally unbiblical and dangerous. In such churches members see each other once a week, sing a few songs, listen to a message, sit beside people who are almost complete strangers, smile politely at those they make eye contact with, and go home. None of this is fellowship, at least not in the way John intends.

Home Groups and Home Churches

Traditionally, many Churches have labeled 'fellowship' as a half-hour of social interaction over a cup of tea or coffee after the service. I grew up in a farming community, and well remember as a child standing outside the Church in the summer, or in a hall in winter, listening to people talking about hay, the weather, price of wool, etc, and occasionally a remark about the sermon, yet most who attended that Church almost never had the opportunity to discuss their faith, problems, or use their spiritual gifts, let alone be involved in mission. The pastor would visit families a few times a year, have a cup of tea, maybe pray, and that was the extent of 'fellowship'.

Sadly, the depth of individual Christian growth amongst such people is minimal, if at all, because Christianity is about living Christ together, finding our gifts and using them, learning to pray and support each other, and recognizing that we 'belong to each other'. This is the concept of *koinonia*, a group of believers who see each other as family and live for each other accordingly.

There are many Churches who have recognized the importance of small groups within a congregation as the key to Biblical fellowship and personal Christian growth. This principle can be seen in action in the very first Christians. In Acts 2:43 we read about that first 3000 Christians who were born again on the Day of Pentecost. Luke tells us that:

They devoted themselves to the apostles' teaching and to the fellowship, to the breaking of bread and to prayer (Acts 2:43).

Is Luke speaking of social activities here, or something far deeper? He answers that question in the following verses, speaking of them having *everything in common*, that they *gave to anyone as he had need,* and *broke bread in their homes and ate together with glad and sincere hearts...*

Notice the obvious references to these people having an understanding of family. They considered themselves as a group to have *everything in common.* These three words are the heart of the word *koinonia.* Not only did they have the Divine nature in common, but they considered that they had everything in common. What did that mean in real terms? It meant that they *gave to anyone as he had need.*

Can we really know the needs of those we are sitting beside in church if we hardly ever speak to them, never pray with them, and have never had a meal with them? But if we are meeting weekly with a small group of believers in a home, then we will soon get to know their needs, and because we are sharing our lives together, recognize them as family.

Family members help each other, and dedicated, loving family members share what they have in common. Sadly, in Western cultures, especially within countries where the majority have salaries which exceed what they need to live on, we have become extremely individualistic, even selfish. Yet Christians in the early Church had the following attitude:

All the believers were one in heart and mind. No one claimed that any of his possessions was his own, but they shared everything they had (Acts 4:32).

And also,

There were no needy persons among them. For from time to time those who owned lands or houses sold them, brought the money from the sales and put it at the apostles' feet, and it was distributed to anyone as he had need (Acts 4:34-35).

When reading such verses I am challenged as to whether I cherish my possessions more than my brothers and sisters in Christ. This is radical Christianity in action, but the reason it is so radical and life-changing is in their recognition of each other as being part of the family of God, children of God, members of one Body of Christ. This kind of giving was not someone foolishly selling their only land or house and making themselves homeless, but rather, people exercising Jesus' warning about storing up wealth (Matthew 6:19-21). They gave of their surplus and saw their possessions as belonging firstly to the Lord, and secondly to each other.

Luke also tells us that they *continued to meet together in the temple courts(Acts 2:46),* and perhaps this is where they listened to the apostles' teaching, but this was no mega church of 3000 plus people who met only one day a week, but rather, many small groups who were living their new faith as a family, meeting in their homes, a family created by the bond of the Spirit, the Body of Christ. This then is the real meaning of *koinonia* when used in terms of fellowship...it is relationship, a recognition that we are bound together and eternally joined in Christ as the children of God.

In my opinion, every Christian who is able should be sharing this form of fellowship with a group of believers. Such groups should never be understood or operated as independent Churches, but rather as intimate units of the Body of Christ and under the authority of overseers. This structure of authority is seen in Luke's words that they *devoted themselves to the apostles' teaching.* These were never small independent groups who refused to submit to apostolic authority, but rather, small home churches, or 'micro-churches' if you prefer, which practiced biblical *koinonia* for the spiritual growth of their members.

There are a great deal of incredibly important areas of spiritual growth which only really manifest themselves within small groups, but firstly a few words about home church structure.

Since 2006 my wife and I have led a home group/church in our small Kiev apartment under the authority of New Life Church. New Life is one of the largest evangelical congregations in Kiev, with about 1,500 members and several pastors. My home group consists regularly of 15-20 Christians who meet weekly, mostly university students and young married couples. My ministry in Ukraine was predominately to university aged students (lecturing in universities), so the home group has naturally formed around this age- group.

One of the advantages of home group/churches is that people of similar ages and stages of life are able to support each other in the specific challenges that face them. For example, university aged people have immediate challenges such as future jobs and marriage partners, and often specific temptations that accompany this stage in life. The home group environment allows an opportunity to walk with them through these challenges and help them to prepare for marriage, parenting, etc.

Home group/churches often naturally form around people of similar life circumstances. For example, a home group/church of mostly young married couples with children gives parents the opportunity to share the challenges specific to this stage of life, help each other in baby-sitting, handing on strollers or other possessions which are no longer needed, etc. This is practical Christianity in action, loving one another through loving acts and seeing each other as family. Let's briefly examine some of the other main areas where home churches aid spiritual growth.

Biblical Study

Studying and knowing God's Word is foundational for spiritual growth. Listening to a sermon once a week and personal devotions are very important, but studying Scripture in an environment where each person can contribute, share inspiration and ask questions, is far more effective in making God's Word inseparable to our daily lives and developing our knowledge and love of Him. In this environment we teach and inspire each other. As a home church leader it is a great encouragement to me to hear weekly testimonies and witness the spiritual growth of people as they study God's Word in depth and apply it to their lives.

Personal Support

Within a regular home church Christians get to know one another deeply. Knowing each other's challenges and temptations, sharing prayer requests, confessing our weaknesses and being dedicated to pray for each other, builds a spiritual bond of true fellowship. Each person understands that they are supported in their walk with the Lord. In 1st Thessalonians 5:11 Paul writes that we must *encourage one another and build each other up.* This kind of personal support is a hallmark of a Christ-centered home group/church. Those who never attend a regular home group often feel isolated when difficulties arise.

Some churches have counselors, or the pastor acts in this capacity, but the troubled Christian may hardly know the pastor, and also, if they have to make an appointment, this is often neglected unless the issue is very serious. In a home church situation it becomes the norm to pray for each other regularly, and this increases trust, provides loving support, and accountability.

Accountability

When Christians realize and begin to live the reality that we belong to Christ, and each other through the Body of Christ, this brings accountability. In 1st Corinthians 12 Paul has a great deal to say about how all Christians are united within the Body of Christ. When one suffers, all suffer (v 26). In Romans 12:5 Paul goes even further stating that *we who are many form one body, and each member belongs to all the others.*

We, as members of the Body of Christ, can no longer claim that we are independent individuals. Yes, we are still individuals and accountable to the Lord, but we are not 'independent'. If we are living in sin, or have health problems, we cannot stand in independence and tell other Christians that 'it's none of your business'. We are accountable to each other because we belong to each other. In a home group/church environment this biblical fact is difficult to ignore, and when taken seriously, through trust and love, is of great benefit.

When we are regularly praying for each other, worshipping together, sharing communion together, studying God's Word and having a meal together, we get to know each other. In this environment there is trust. People share their weaknesses and temptations, their testimonies of over-coming, and those who have been through the same offer empathy and support. We become accountable to each other in Christ.

Opportunities for Ministry and Mission

In congregations which do not have home group/churches, there are few opportunities for members to develop and exercise several areas of spiritual gifts and talents. Usually, the best musicians play in the worship team, the best singers lead worship, the trained teachers and pastors give the message, and many who long to use their gifts live in frustration. Home groups open opportunities for all members to discover, develop and exercise their gifts and talents, and this naturally leads to the group reaching out in mission to neighbors and unsaved friends.

The home church in my apartment has musicians, singers, prayer warriors, teachers, cooks, potential pastors, evangelists etc. All learn the foundational role of servant-hood, most discover their spiritual gifts, and all are involved in one ministry or other. Many of them discover a desire to study Scripture and theology in an even deeper way and go on to become home church leaders themselves. As a home group/church leader, it is exciting to witness young people discovering their gifts, taking a weekly responsibility to use those gifts in service to each other and unbelievers, and going on to become servant leaders themselves.

Summary

The categories above are just some of the ways that home group/churches develop spiritual growth, but the most important and observable growth is in love, both for the Lord Jesus Christ, and for each other. Home churches are about worshipping the Lord together, studying His word together, sharing communion together, praying for each other, sharing a weekly meal together, and supporting each other through the trials of life. This is true *koinonia*, true fellowship, something that all Christians should be involved in throughout their earthly lives, for it is something we will continue for all eternity.

Study Four

The Second Mark: Confession

1st John 1:7-10

7 But if we walk in the light, as he is in the light, we have fellowship with one another, and the blood of Jesus, his Son, purifies us from all sin. 8 If we claim to be without sin, we deceive ourselves and the truth is not in us. 9 If we confess our sins, he is faithful and just and will forgive us our sins and purify us from all unrighteousness. 10 If we claim we have not sinned, we make him out to be a liar and his word has no place in our lives.

In this study we will discuss the importance of recognizing the continuing existence of our fallen natures, the need for sincere confession when we fall into sins, and the fact that Christ will always forgive us and help us to take up our cross and continue our walk with Him.

But firstly, please note that, as in the first few verses of his letter, where John emphasizes the reality of Jesus earthly body, here in verse 7 he draws our attention to the blood of Jesus, the very life-force of the Savior which was poured out for sinful humanity. Jesus death was real, his sacrifice on the cross was no Docetist deception, for unless He was a real man who bled and died, He cannot purify us from all sin.

However, here John reminds us of the blood of Christ, not to condemn Docetism, but to point us to the cross, the place where sin was dealt with forever, the place of atonement, forgiveness, and new life. When we take our eyes off the cross, even for a short time, when we lay down our cross and try to continue our walk without its constant reminder, our old, sinful, fallen natures try to lead us off the narrow path.

All Christians can be led astray by both false teachings and sinful practices. This does not mean that they have lost their salvation, for the fact of the indwelling Spirit is a guarantee of salvation (Ephesians 1:14), rather it means that fellowship with the Lord and Church is seriously affected. True fellowship, unaffected by both false teachings or sin, is John's intentions for writing to the Church.

There are those who teach that John is speaking of non-christians in these verses and calling them to repentance. This erroneous teaching comes from a gross misunderstanding of chapter 3 where John claims that those who are born of God can no longer continue to sin (3:6,9). We will examine chapter 3 in Study Nine in order to understand John's claims, however, John makes it very clear who he is addressing in the above verses as he refers to these ones as *'My dear children' (2:1).*

Prior to salvation we walked in darkness, we were ignorant of the holiness of God and slaves to our sinful natures (Romans 6). Yet we were not completely ignorant of the holiness of God as we are creatures made in His image, and all human beings have a conscience (Romans 1 and 2) and a fundamental understanding of right and wrong, of morality and justice. Yet we *chose* to walk in darkness as those who walk in rebellion to the demands of holiness, we chose to walk our own way and refused to submit to our Creator.

When the Holy Spirit brought illumination of our sinful state, we fell down before the cross of Christ and confessed our utterly hopeless state of sinfulness. Some of us may have tried to live a moral life devoid of the transforming power of the Holy Spirit, and failed at every turn, for those who are slaves to sin are slaves indeed. Only Christ can set the prisoner free.

When we surrendered our wills to His will, crying out for forgiveness, He *purified us from all sin* and gave us His declaration and status of perfection (Hebrews 10:14). We were no longer slaves to sin, for now His power and passion for holiness dwelt within us, His nature was joined to our own.

But our old nature and its ungodly habits remained in us. The sinful nature is fundamentally sinful, it continues to desire to sin and, therefore, we can never *claim to be without sin,* indeed, the closer we come to Christ the more we recognize our sinfulness.

8 If we claim to be without sin, we deceive ourselves and the truth is not in us. 9 If we confess our sins, he is faithful and just and will forgive us our sins and purify us from all unrighteousness. 10 If we claim we have not sinned, we make him out to be a liar and his word has no place in our lives.

As Christians we live in a constant battle within, a battle between our Divine and fallen natures. The old nature tries to hide in the shadows of our newly illuminated souls, telling us we cannot live without those old habits. These are the 'sins', which have their roots in the old nature, that John is reminding us of. In regards to salvation these sins are already forgiven in Christ, but in terms of our fellowship with Him they must be confessed and abandoned for us to be continually cleansed from all unrighteousness. So why do I call this one of the marks of a true Christian?

Those who have been born again cannot live in the joy of the Spirit whilst harboring unconfessed sin. The sinful Christian is the most miserable of people, for the indwelling Spirit will continue to convict constantly. The non-christian may have a twinge of guilt and ignore his conscience, but the born again person no longer has this option, for the light of Christ continually illuminates the shadows where sinful desires dwell.

A Christian may try to ignore the Holy Spirit, and sear his conscience in the process, but if this person was ever truly born of the Spirit, then the Spirit will eventually bring him to repentance. The true Christian confesses and repents, he turns away from the sin, for within him is the same passion and desire for holiness which is the character of God. The passion for holiness, which is a part of all true Christians, drives the child of God to his knees, whereas the non-christian can happily live in darkness.

Confession and Repentance

Confession is much more than an admission of guilt. A person may admit their guilt and yet have no intention of turning away from sin, rather, they find excuses to justify their behavior. Confession must always be accompanied with repentance and faith. Repentance is to turn away, or change one's mind; it is a decision to trust the Lord for His power to live according to His will, to turn away from sin, take up our cross again and follow Him. True repentance is to forsake our sin and walk in the opposite direction away from that sin, taking up our cross and following our Lord. We know that we have His power to achieve this, for we experienced that power when we were born again. As Peter tells us:

His divine power has given us everything we need for life and godliness through our knowledge of him who called us by his own glory and goodness (2nd Peter 1:3).

Event and Process

In Mark 8:34 Jesus taught that if any would come after Him, he must *deny himself, take up his cross and follow*. There are three stages spoken of here.

The first is self denial. The heart of the unbeliever is self in the center, self on the throne. When the Holy Spirit convicts the unsaved of sin, the person is ready to deny self and to say 'not my will, but yours be done'. Surrender to the Lordship of Christ is essential for salvation (Colossians 2:6).

The second step is to take up our cross. The cross is a symbol of death. In the case of salvation it is death to our ego or the self-ruling principle, something Paul explains in depth in Romans 6. In Greek, the word we translate as 'I', is *ego.* When Paul writes in Galatians 2:20, *I have been crucified with Christ, it is no longer I who lives, but Christ who lives in me,* he is speaking of the death of his ego, that principle that demanded to live in its own will, a will in rebellion to God.

The self-ruling ego must die. Without this death there is no need to be 'born again'. This is not merely an analogy, but an existential experience of death and new birth. The sinful nature and ego are not the same thing. The ego, or self-ruling principle, dies, and with that death, the Divine Nature takes it place as the authority within the believer. It is these two natures which war within the believer, but as Paul tells us, we have no obligation to our sinful nature to live according to it (Romans 8:12).

The third step is to follow, to be a disciple, to walk as Jesus walked. In Luke 9:23 we can read the parallel verse to Mark 8:34, however, Luke adds one word, he says we must take up our cross 'daily'.

Salvation is both event and process. We call the process sanctification, and the way we go about that process is in daily self-denial, taking up our cross to follow our Lord in the same way through which we submitted to Him in the beginning. Although our ego has been crucified with Christ, our old sin nature, which was fuelled by our ego, remains. That nature must be constantly submitted to the Divine nature which now governs our life.

At times Christians allow their sin nature to rise up, we fail to deny our sin natures, we lay down our cross and fall into various sins. The Holy Spirit convicts us at these times, He calls us to gaze upon the cross of Christ, confess our sins, take up our cross and continue our journey of faith.

Some teach that, during the period of sin and confession, a person has forfeit their salvation. This is a false teaching which ends up drawing our attention away from the work of Christ on the cross and onto our performance as Christians. This teaching also denies one of the most fundamental of all Christian doctrines, namely, grace.

Grace

In Romans 6 the apostle Paul discusses the issues of sin and grace in the life of a Christian, and in the next chapter he uses an analogy from marriage. In these chapters he is addressing Jewish Christians in Rome, men who knew the Law of Moses (Romans 7:1) and were struggling to understand their moral responsibilities now that they were no longer under the law. In Romans 5 Paul explains how death entered the world through the sin of Adam, and how the death of Christ has brought new life. Near the end of the chapter Paul explains that *the law was added so that the trespass might increase.* He goes on to say that where sin increased, so grace increased all the more, *so also grace might reign through righteousness to bring eternal life through Jesus Christ our Lord* (v20-21).

Paul is contrasting the reign of death through sin, and the reign of grace through the righteousness of Christ. Adam was not under the law, therefore, he didn't sin under the law. His sin, which brought death to all, *because all sinned,* was a single act of disobedience. The law increased the trespass because it contained over 600 commands, hundreds of laws which increased the trespass of those who broke them. Paul is telling these Christians that grace through the death of Christ increased to cover all of these trespasses, and thus the reason for the question, *shall we go on sinning that grace may increase* (6:1), shall we add more sins to receive more grace?

Paul's answer is a definitive 'no'! He goes on to explain that Christians are baptized into the very death of Christ, buried with Him in baptism, and raised to live a new life in Him. Now that we live in Christ death has *no mastery over us*, so we should *count ourselves dead to sin but alive to God in Christ Jesus.* He tells the Roman Christians:

Do not offer the parts of your body to sin, as instruments of wickedness, but rather offer yourselves to God, as those who have been brought from death to life; and offer the parts of your body to him as instruments of righteousness. For sin shall not be your master, because you are not under law, but under grace (Romans 6:13-14).

Those who teach that a Christian can lose their salvation through an act of sin have no understanding, or simply refuse to believe, what Paul is saying here. We are not under the law, not under a penalty of death, but rather we live *under grace*. This message was too good to be true for some, and such is the reason the apostle anticipated the question about continuing to sin so that grace might increase. Paul was never suggesting that grace is a license for sin, but he wanted his readers to understand without doubt that the law no longer applied to them, they were free from it, had died to it, and now could live in the joy and freedom of grace.

To further explain his point Paul uses an analogy from the covenant of marriage (Romans 7:1-6). He tells them that *the law has authority over a man only as long as he lives.* Paul then explains that the law is like the law of marriage, it is 'till death do us part'. A man or woman is bound to their spouse until their spouse dies, only then are they free to marry another.

For Paul, the law was our spouse! We were bound to it until either it, or we, died. Paul has just spent most of chapter six explaining that death, a death that meant we were free to be joined to another, to Christ, as His bride. In chapter 7: 4-6, Paul explains to his readers,

4 So, my brothers, you also died to the law through the body of Christ, that you might belong to another, to him who was raised from the dead, in order that we might bear fruit to God. 5 For when we were controlled by the sinful nature (flesh), the sinful passions aroused by the law were at work in our bodies, so that we bore fruit for death. 6 But now, by dying to what once bound us, we have been released from the law so that we serve in the new way of the Spirit, and not in the old way of the written code (Romans 7:4-6).

This powerful analogy should be enough to convince every Christian that we are free from the law, free to live and serve Christ under the new way of the Spirit, yet there are many today, who, like the Roman Jews, refuse to fully embrace the grace of God through faith in Christ. Perhaps the fault lies at the feet of those who claim that a person is born again through a simple confession of belief in Christ, rather than explaining that discipleship demands denial of self, the taking up of our cross, and walking with Christ. Is it possible that there are many within congregations who are not regenerate, people who have never experienced death to self and rebirth?

If the answer to that question is yes, if congregations have unregenerate members, as the parables of the sheep and goats, and wheat and tares confirm, then such people are still under the law and can only produce *fruit for death*. Such people are often those who claim that they have no sin. Such a person lives as a religious hypocrite. His life is full of shadows. He puts on a religious face, pretends to walk in the light, but secretly loves the darkness. Such a person is still a slave to sin and has no fellowship with God.

Summary

As Christians, it is not our role to hunt down and expose the goats or tares within our congregations. Our priority, in the context of this study, is self-examination. We should ask ourselves the following questions:

1. Am I able to happily live with the sins I commit, or does the Holy Spirit within me drive me to my knees in sincere confession, longing to be *purified from all sin*? If the former, then it is very doubtful that I have died with Christ, if the latter, then this is one of John's proofs that the Spirit has given me new birth.

2. Am I still living in fear of the wrath of God, or living in the joy of the freedom of His grace and motivated by love for Him. If the former, then either I have been mislead about grace, or have never truly experienced it. John tells us in chapter four of this letter that *there is no fear in love. But perfect love drives out fear, because fear has to do with punishment. The man who fears is not made perfect in love (4:18)*.

The Lord desires that we live in His love, motivated by the unconditional grace we have received through the sacrifice of Jesus Christ. The Lord desires that we walk in fellowship with Him, and we can only do this through honest confession and repentance.

The challenge to us is this: Are we trying to hide sinful habits in the shadows of our souls? Are there parts of our lives which we do not want the Lord to illuminate, desires and practices which we know are unrighteous, things for which we are ashamed? Let us not pretend that we are not still sinners, for to do so is to call Christ a liar, for *if we claim to be without sin, we deceive ourselves and the truth is not in us..*

He calls us to bring our sins into the light, to confess them, and He promises to forgive us and cleanse us from all unrighteousness. We need not live with shame, we have only to leave our sinful burden at the cross as we daily carry our cross. Failing to confess and accept forgiveness will rob a Christian of close fellowship with the Lord and destroy the joy and peace which comes from being cleansed.

Study Five

The Third Mark: Obedience

1st John 2:1-8

2:1 My dear children, I write this to you so that you will not sin. But if anyone does sin, we have one who speaks to the Father in our defense - Jesus Christ, the Righteous One. 2 He is the atoning sacrifice for our sins, and not only for ours but also for the sins of the whole world. 3 We know that we have come to know him if we obey his commandments.

4 The man who says "I know him," but does not do what he commands is a liar, and the truth is not in him. 5 But if anyone obeys his word, God's love is truly made complete in him. This is how we know we are in him: 6 Whoever claims to live in him must walk as Jesus did.

In this study we will examine the third mark of a true Christian, namely obedience to Christ. But firstly, we see John qualifying his previous instructions regarding the sins which Christians commit. In Romans 6:1-7 the apostle Paul anticipates the reaction of those who find it difficult to accept the full extent of God's grace in Christ. They argued that if grace covers all sin, then what is to stop a person from sinning, for surely an increase of sin brings an increase of grace.

I believe that John is addressing the same issue here. In the previous verses he has told his 'dear children' that if they claim to be without sin then they deceive themselves, and he gives instructions to confess such sins to Christ who will purify us from all unrighteousness. Some might argue that this teaching of grace may encourage some to think they have a license to sin. John answers this criticism with saying that he writes these things so that we *will not sin*, however, if anyone falls to sin we have the One who *speaks to the Father in our defense - Jesus Christ the Righteous One.*

Before examining the third mark of obedience, let us briefly discuss what John means when he speaks of Christ as the one who defends us.

Christ: Our Defender

John calls Jesus Christ the 'atoning sacrifice' (NIV) or 'propitiation for sins', the One who removes the wrath of God from us. Jesus Christ is our defense (*parakletos*). This word is used in a legal sense as of the one who defends us before a magistrate. John's message is this: 'I write to you to remind you that sin still dwells within all of us in our sinful natures. To deny this is to call Christ a liar. I write to encourage you to fight against sin, to despise it and confess it, but if you fall, remember that our Lord Jesus Christ stands to defend us before the holy throne of our Heavenly Father.'

In some cases the advocate (lawyer) for the defense may be pleading the case of an innocent person, but in this case the accused is guilty. Christ does not plead our innocence, but *His righteousness* on our behalf. In other words, He stands, not only as advocate, but as mediator and substitute. The shed blood of Christ has paid for the sins of humanity, all of humanity, *He is the atoning sacrifice for our sins, and not only for ours but also for the sins of the whole world,* (v2) for all time.

This claim of John's, along with other verses within the NT, completely refutes the Calvinist doctrine of Limited Atonement. According to this false doctrine, Christ's atoning sacrifice is only for those who have been predestined, or predetermined to salvation. Such a notion defames the character of Christ who healed all who came to Him, who fed the twenty thousand, who never turned away any sinner.

But John's theology is not a statement of universal salvation, that all are saved, but rather, an invitation and promise, that as Christ proclaimed; *But , when I am lifted up from the earth, will draw all men to myself.* As the apostle Peter wrote, God is patient:

...not wanting anyone to perish, but everyone to come to repentance (2nd Peter 3:9).

Therefore, those who belong to Him are *in Christ* (Colossians 3:3) and are covered *by* Christ. Jesus Christ is our representative; He is the Righteous One who has been *tempted in every way, just as we are - yet was without sin (Hebrews 4:15).* The writer to the Hebrews tells us that Christ can sympathize with our weakness, and that we can:

...approach the throne of grace with confidence, so that we may receive mercy and find grace to help us in our time of need (4:16).

We have all the help we need. We have the indwelling Holy Spirit who gives us both a hatred for sin and power to resist, therefore, we make every effort to live without sin, but receive grace and mercy if we fail sometimes in the battle.

The Third Mark: Obedience

From verses three to six John then outlines what I have called the 'third mark' of a true Christian.

3 We know that we have come to know him if we obey his commandments. 4 The man who says "I know him", but does not do what he commands is a liar, and the truth is not in him. 5 But if anyone obeys his word, God's love is truly made complete in him. This is how we know we are in him: 6 Whoever claims to live in him must walk as Jesus did.

John uses the word 'know' four times in this short passage. There are forms of knowledge which simply add to our general knowledge or understanding of something or someone, but the knowledge of God John speaks of here is knowledge which has a fundamental effect on our behavior.

Knowing God is not, as the Gnostics taught, a form of mysticism or intellectual understanding, rather, it is a knowledge which transforms the way in which we live, as it is tied to our relationship with Jesus Christ. The Lord used the analogy of a shepherd to explain this relationship in John 10:14-15:

"I am the good shepherd; I know my sheep and my sheep know me - just as the Father knows me and I know the Father - and I lay down my life for the sheep."

In study two we saw that the word 'fellowship' (*koinonia*) comes from the same Greek root as 'partaker'. Those who know Christ are partakers of the Divine nature and have intimate fellowship with God. The indwelling Spirit brings to us the desire for all that is of God; His holiness, truth, and the desire to walk in obedience to His word.

Jesus, while He was on this earth, is the perfect example of this truth. He said that He came to do the will of His Father (John 6:38), for their wills are inseparable, their fellowship indivisible. If *our* wills are contrary to the will of God, then we do not know God, are not bound to Him in fellowship, and are not partakers of His Divine nature.

It is not possible to be united with Christ, to have been filled with the Holy Spirit, and have no desire to obey His word. This is why John writes that *anyone who says "I know Him", but does not do as he commands is a liar and the truth is not in him.*

The New Covenant

The Day of Pentecost recorded in Acts 2 describes the inauguration of the new covenant, the day when the Holy Spirit came to dwell within those who believed that Jesus was the Christ. John's statement about *knowing Him* echoes the words of Jeremiah 31:33-34 which speaks of the new covenant, a passage quoted in Hebrews 8:10-12;

'This is the covenant I will make with the house of Israel after that time,' declares the Lord. 'I will put my law in their minds and write it on their hearts. I will be

51

their God, and they will be my people. No longer will a man teach his neighbor, saying, 'Know the Lord,' because they will all know me, from the least of them to the greatest, declares the Lord. 'For I will forgive their wickedness and will remember their sins no more.'

The Old Testament history of the Jewish people leaves us in no doubt that Israel failed miserably in trying to keep the commands of God. Only those chosen as prophets, and anointed kings like David, would have claimed to really know God, the rest lived in fear of His wrath, or disregarded the covenant and worshipped false gods. The Holy Spirit was upon the prophets, guiding their words and actions, but the vast majority of the people never experienced the Holy Spirit's presence, so God remained as a stranger to them in terms of relationship.

Their relationship with God was connected to the law, the 600 commands given through Moses, but those who are not filled with the Spirit (born again) remain slaves to their sin natures and are powerless to fulfill God's commands. Yes, they might be successful in never committing murder, adultery or stealing, but what of coveting, or of having no other gods, or loving the Lord with all their hearts, minds, etc, and most importantly, what of faith? Can anyone who doesn't know God place their faith in Him?

Moses led the Jews out of Egypt after various miraculous plagues, the presence of God was with them day and night as they walked through the Red Sea, were fed with manna and quail, received the law at Sinai and came to the Promised Land. But only two out of about two million had enough faith to trust God and go against the fierce inhabitants of Canaan. By this time they knew quite a lot about God, but they didn't know Him intimately, as they were not 'partakers' of His Spirit.

Paul tells us in Galatians 3:24-25 that *the law was put in charge to lead us to Christ that we might be justified by faith. Now that faith has come, we are no longer under the supervision of the law.*

Paul goes on to explain in chapter 4 that we have become children of God, adopted into His family *because God sent the Spirit of his Son into our hearts, the Spirit who calls out "Abba, Father".*

As Christians, our relationship with our Heavenly Father becomes something akin to the relationship Jesus had with His Father whilst on this earth, and this is why John reminds us that if we claim to be in Christ, we must obey His commands and *walk as Jesus did.*

What does He command?

If we were to approach the answer to the question above in terms of the Old Covenant, we could search the gospels and find over fifty commands from Jesus. The Sermon on the Mount (Matthew 5,6,7) is a good example of this, however, it is my conviction that Jesus' intention was never to lay down a new or revised version of the Mosaic Law, but rather to show, in a general sense, that firstly, no person (other than He) can keep the law, and secondly, that God seeks worshippers in Spirit and Truth rather than rules and regulations.

Throughout the Sermon on the Mount we see Jesus using the phrase, *'you have heard it said', and 'you have read', 'but I tell you'.* Jesus' message is that even if you think you are keeping the Law outwardly, you have not changed within. For example, we may pat ourselves on the back for not physically committing adultery, but we have already gone through the lustful process of committing it in fantasy within our hearts. Jesus summarizes what he has taught thus far in Matthew 5:48 with the words *'be perfect, therefore, as your Heavenly Father is perfect'*.

Perfection! What a standard!

Over the next two chapters of Matthew Jesus continues to challenge his listeners in regards to prayer, fasting, storing up wealth, worrying, judging others, etc, and finally He brings us to the conclusion. He tells us to *'ask, seek and knock'*, gives an illustration of a father giving good gifts to his children, and speaks of the narrow gate. What gift is He speaking of? The answer to that is found in the parallel verses of Luke 11:9-13 which ends, *how much more will your Father in heaven give the Holy Spirit to those who ask Him'*.

The key to living in obedience to Christ is in being united to Him through becoming partakers of the Divine nature. Jesus commands us to be born again (John 3:3), an event which begins with denying self and taking up our cross, and continues on a daily basis as sanctification whilst following Him (Luke 9:23). If we have experienced this event, and live in the transforming process of sanctification, then His command to 'be perfect' becomes a reality, for we are covered by His perfection as we live for Him.

Hebrews 10:14 expresses this beautifully, speaking of the sacrifice of Christ and what it has achieved for those who have committed their lives to Him, stating, *because by one sacrifice he has made perfect forever those who are being made holy'.* Christ has made us perfect by His righteousness, as we are in Him, and we, in our fallen bodies, continue to become what He has declared us to be, holy.

This status, or declaration of perfection, is gifted to all who are born again, for we live within the perfection of Christ, covered by His perfect blood, and empowered by His Spirit to live in obedience to Him.

When Christ is within, His will becomes our will, His obedient life to the Father becomes that which we desire, and the Holy Spirit sets about transforming us to live in that obedience. All of this comes about because we 'know Him'. He lives within us, guiding our steps, convicting us when we turn towards sin, calling us to repent when we fall, and motivating us through our mutual love to persevere.

Obeying the commands of Christ is all about Christ, and we knowing Christ. We do not need a list of rules and regulations because He advises at every decision and convicts when we disobey His voice within.

The letters of the Apostles are full of this teaching, but also, warnings to those Christians who have either failed to obey His voice, or allowed their conscience to be seared through continual sin. The role of pastors and teachers, as well as the New Testament Scriptures, is not to give us lists of rules, but rather to continually remind us to live in obedience through being led by the Spirit for *if you are led by the Spirit, you are not under law (Galatians 5:18).*

Summary

A person may know much *about* Jesus Christ, they may have studied the Bible and biblical history for years, they may even have a theological degree, but if they do not obey Him they do not 'know Him', as John defines 'knowing'. Likewise, a person may say that they love Jesus Christ and still not know Him. Some people say that they love what Jesus taught, that He was a great teacher and humanitarian, a man that told us to love our neighbors. They see Him as a social reformer and claim to love everything He stood for, yet they refuse to submit to Him as Lord and receive Him as Savior. Such people are still driven by their own ego, are slaves to sin and, ultimately, they remain enemies of God.

To know Jesus Christ is to love Jesus Christ, and to love Him is to obey His commands. Jesus stated that *if you obey my commands, you will remain in my love, just as I have obeyed my Father's commands and remain in his love (John 15:10).*

In John 15:12 Jesus says: *My command is this: Love each other as I have loved you.* This command sums up the teaching of Jesus and is well-known, but this primary command is impossible for those who have not been born again. This command includes the command to *love our enemies and to pray for those who persecute us (Matt 5:44)*, it includes the command to *take up our cross and follow Him (Mark 8:34)*, it includes the command to *be perfect, therefore, as your Heavenly Father is perfect (Matt 5:48).*

None of these commands are possible for unregenerate fallen humanity, they are only possible for those who are joined to the One who commands, the

One who loves His enemies, who took up the cross, and is perfect as our Heavenly Father is perfect.

John's message is both an encouragement and warning. For those who truly know Christ, both the power and desire to obey Him have become a part of who we are, for the Divine nature dwells within us. His power to obey, and desire and love of holiness, become a part of us when we become 'new creations' (2nd Corinthians 5:17).

This is what it means to be re-born, born from above, regenerated. When we obey His word His love is made complete in us, it is fulfilled in us, and we live it as an existential reality. This is the joy that Christ spoke of, the joy of being in God's will, free from the slavery that bound us to sin, and free to live as children of God.

And it is a warning to those who do not obey the commands of Christ. They do not obey because they do not know Him, do not love Him, and are not filled with His passion for holiness; the *truth is not in them*.

John challenges us to examine ourselves regarding our claim that we know Jesus Christ. The mark of a true Christian is obedience to the truth that dwells within us, for Christ is the Way, Truth and Life. If we do not possess the same passion for holiness that Jesus possessed, then we should ask ourselves if we possess the Spirit of the Lord or are His possession.

Study Six

The Fourth Mark: Practical Love

1st John 2:7-11 and 3:11-18

7 Dear friends, I am not writing you a new commandment but an old one, which you have had since the beginning. This old command is the message you have heard. 8 Yet I am writing you a new command; its truth is seen in him and you, because the darkness is passing and the true light is already shining. 9 Anyone who claims to be in the light but hates his brother is still in the darkness.

10 Whoever loves his brother lives in the light, and there is nothing in him to make him stumble. 11 But whoever hates his brother is in the darkness and walks around in the darkness; he does not know where he is going, because the darkness has blinded him.

In our previous study we alluded to Jesus' command to love each other as He has loved us. I suggested that this primary command could not be obeyed without new birth, for the natural man is incapable of walking in the light of love. In the verses we are studying here, John takes this even further.

Please note that we are using two passages in John's letter regarding the topic of love within the Body of Christ. Unlike the apostle Paul, who writes in a very systematic way, building on one theme towards another, John's letter often comes back to the same topics again, therefore, we will begin in chapter two and conclude in the next chapter.

7 Dear friends, I am not writing you a new commandment but an old one, which you have had since the beginning. This old command is the message you have heard.

Firstly, what does John mean by the message we *have had since the beginning*? The answer to that is in 3:11-18:

This is the message you heard from the beginning: We should love one another. 12 Do not be like Cain, who belonged to the evil one and murdered his brother. And why did he murder him? Because his own actions were evil and his brother's were righteous. 13 Do not be surprised my brothers, if the world hates you. 14 We know we have passed from death to life, because we love our brothers. Anyone who does not love remains in death. 15 Anyone who hates his brother is a murderer, and you know that no murderer has eternal life in him.

16 This is how we know what love is: Jesus Christ laid down his life for us. And we ought to lay down our lives for our brothers. 17 If anyone has material possessions and sees his brother in need but has no pity on him, how can the love of God be in him? 18 Dear children, let us not love with words or tongue but with actions and in truth.

John takes us right back to the first generation of humanity. He is about to speak of loving our brothers in Christ, but he takes us back to the first two brothers who ever lived, brothers who should have had love for each other. John reminds us that Cain murdered his brother Abel. Abel had brought an appropriate offering to the Lord and received a blessing, but Cain brought what *he* pleased and received no favor from the Lord (Genesis 4:2-10).

The Lord told him that if he did *what was right* he would be accepted, and warned him that sin was crouching at his door and desired to master him. Cain ignored the Lord and murdered his brother. When questioned about where Abel was, Cain's reply was, "I don't know. Am I my brother's keeper?" This answer was paramount in saying "I am not my brother's keeper."

Cain's reply teaches us the Biblical concepts of hatred and love. There are several Greek words translated as love within the New Testament, but the word John is using here is *agape,* the same word Paul uses to describe God's love in 1st Corinthians 13:4-8, and John states of God in 1st John 4:16.

To love (*agape*) is to act in love towards someone, but to hate is to have no care for the welfare of another. Cain's hatred also brought the emotion of anger and was manifested in the act of murder, but his answer showed that he didn't care about what he had done.

In the New Testament the word hate (*miseo*) is used by Jesus to speak about what we care about in Luke 14. He tells us that unless we hate our mother, father, children etc, we cannot be His disciples, and likewise He says we cannot serve two masters for we will hate one and love the other. The primary meaning of hate being used here is to neglect. Christ is using the term in the sense of what we care about and what we neglect; He is telling us that to care for family or money above God is to neglect or hate God.

If we care about family more than following Christ, then family have become an idol which prevents us from having Him in the center of our lives and experiencing new birth. He is not commanding us to neglect our immediate families, but rather that we are neglecting God Himself in preference to family. If, in order to have Christ in the very center we must turn our backs on family, if that is the price of becoming disciples, then this we must do, otherwise, we remain in the same darkness as them.

Likewise, John tells us that he who loves his brother has passed from death to life, but he who hates his brother remains in death. As Christians, we cannot say, as Cain did, that we are not our brother's keeper. Love for a brother is a love which acts through loving actions towards our brother, the same kind of love that God expresses when we read John 3:16 that *God so loved the world that He gave His only Son.* This is *agape* love.

When we bring the teachings of Jesus and John together the conclusion is as follows. In order to be united with Christ and experience the agape love that regeneration brings, we must place our new birth as our first priority, not neglecting those we love, but understanding that we do not love them as Christ loves them until we are united with Him. One of the proofs that regeneration has occurred is in the manifestation of agape love. If this particular type of love, a love which defines God, is absent, then most likely new birth is also absent, and the person remains in death.

John has told us previously that true fellowship is the union of our lives with Christ and each other *in*

Christ, therefore, we who are united can never answer as Cain did, 'am I my brother's keeper?' Our brother in Christ is as Christ to us, his welfare is our welfare, we love him as Christ loves him, we care as Christ cares. If that love does not exist we are still in darkness, for it is the absence of loving action and responsibility which defines New Testament hate. In the next verses of chapter three John now defines agape love as it relates to loving each other.

16 This is how we know what love is: Jesus Christ laid down his life for us. And we ought to lay down our lives for our brothers. 17 If anyone has material possessions and sees his brother in need but has no pity on him, how can the love of God be in him? 18 Dear children, let us not love with words or tongue but with actions and in truth.

John points us to Jesus Christ as the ultimate expression of agape love in action, and challenges us to have the same willingness to sacrifice ourselves for each other. From first glance we may say that John is suggesting that we must be willing to die in our brother's place, if called to, and he may have this in mind. Such would be an extreme and unlikely circumstance, but he makes it very clear in verse 17, speaking of our material possessions, what is expected from us on a daily basis. John is telling us that we should view our Christian brothers and sisters as we would our immediate natural family.

Paul tells us that *if anyone does not provide for his relatives, and especially for his immediate family, he has denied the faith and is worse than an unbeliever (1st Timothy 5:8).*

Unbelievers consider it a natural thing to provide for their blood relatives, but John wants us to understand that our spiritual brothers and sisters are our true relatives, eternal relatives. If we do not act in love towards those we are joined to in Christ, then how can we say that the love of God is in us? As well as this, Christ would have us also show agape love to complete strangers, for such is His message in the parable of the Good Samaritan when answering the question "who is my neighbor?" (Luke 10:25-37).

Agape love is fundamental to the Divine Nature. It is a love which acts towards others, it is the love which drove Jesus Christ to the cross, it is that perfect love which God showed in sending His Son to die for us whilst we were still His enemies (Romans 5:8). If we claim to know Jesus Christ and be united with Him, then this love will be manifest in our lives, firstly towards our brothers and sisters in Christ, and even to those who are our spiritual enemies.

And finally, a few words on John's statement in verse 15.

15 Anyone who hates his brother is a murderer, and you know that no murderer has eternal life in him.

Keeping in mind that the word hate means to neglect to act, consider the following example. You are standing on a noisy platform waiting for your train when you see a blind man walking towards the tracks. He seems to be unaware that the train is approaching at speed, yet you take no action to prevent him from falling off the platform to his death. This too is the New Testament meaning of hate. We who know Christ realize that there are many people around us walking in darkness, blind to the eternal life which is available to them.

Is John suggesting that those who claim to be Christians, yet do nothing to help others find Christ, are actually murderers in their hearts, people devoid of the love of God which acts to save us from eternal death? Is this not the fundamental meaning of Jesus' message in His discourse on the Sheep and Goats from Matthew 25:31-46? In this context, one does not have to act to be considered a murderer in the way that Cain acted, but rather to fail to act in love. This is the context in which John uses the word 'hate'.

Summary

The presence and manifestation of agape love is one of the marks of a true Christian. As John states, it is not simply a love of *words and tongue,* but love which acts towards our brothers and sisters in need, and compels us to share the gospel with those who remain in darkness. Jesus explained the difference between the sheep, His true children, and goats, religious hypocrites, in Matthew 25:31-46. The sheep acted in love, feeding the hungry, inviting strangers into their homes, clothing the poor, caring for the sick and visiting prisoners. They did this out of love, compelled by the Spirit of Christ to act as Christ acts.

But the goats never even noticed the hungry, poor, homeless, sick or imprisoned. Their neglect amounted to 'hate', and in their inaction, they proved that agape love was absent in their lives. In the case of agape love we can say that 'actions speak louder than words'. If we are not manifesting agape love through selfless, loving actions, then we should seriously examine ourselves as to whether or not the God who is Love is living within us.

Study Seven

The Fifth Mark: Not of this World

1st John 2:12-17

12 I write to you, dear children, because your sins have been forgiven on account of his name. 13 I write to you, fathers, because you have known him who is from beginning. I write to you, young men, because you have overcome the evil one. I write to you, dear children, because you have known the Father.

14 I write to you, fathers, because you have known him who is from the beginning. I write to you, young men, because you are strong, and the word of God lives in you, and you have overcome the evil one.

15 Do not love the world or anything in the world. If anyone loves the world, the love of the Father is not in him. 16 For everything in the world - the cravings of sinful man, the lust of his eyes, and the boasting of what he has and does - comes not from the Father but from the world. 17 The world and its desires pass away, but the man who does the will of God lives forever.

John begins this section with some words of encouragement which lead into his comments about the world. Firstly, those who use Greek will see that he uses two tenses, 'I write' and 'I wrote' (2:13). When speaking of his time of writing, John uses 'I write', but when anticipating those who will read the letter he uses 'I wrote'. He is not referring to a previous letter here.

Secondly, John uses three titles to his readers, 'dear children', (or little children and little sons) fathers, and young men. The *dear children* is a general expression denoting those who are the children of God, adopted into His family (they *know the Father)* and are *forgiven on account of his name*, the name of Jesus. The *fathers* are those who have been longest in the faith, and some of them have known Jesus whilst He was here on this earth. The fathers are characterized by knowledge, whereas the *young men* by activity.

His comments to young men as *overcomers* is seen as an encouragement to those who have submitted youthful passions to the will of God in Christ, overcoming, not by their own strength, but because *the word of God* lives in them. 'Overcome' is a word John uses frequently, a word he also knew from Jesus' lips (John 16:33) where the Lord gave His disciples hope for their future because He had *overcome the world.* All of those he encourages in these verses have overcome the world through their knowledge of and willingness to overcome the world as Christ did.

We now come to John's instructions concerning the 'world'. As Jesus has shown throughout His earthly life, we are also called to overcome the world as He did, through His strength which dwells within us, a daily dependence on Him. John's opening statement tells us not to love the world or anything in the world.

15 Do not love the world or anything in the world. If anyone loves the world, the love of the Father is not in him.

In the previous study we examined the word love, but before we can begin to understand John's command here, we need to define what he means by the word 'world'. The word John uses for 'world' is the Greek *Kosmos*. This word is generally used in three ways throughout the New Testament.

Firstly, to refer to the physical world, the creation. Secondly, to refer to the system and ideologies of the world which stand in rebellion to God's will. In this sense Satan is called the 'prince of this world' (John12:31, 14:30, 16:11) for he is the one leading the rebellion.

Thirdly, the word is used to refer to the people of the world as in John 3:16 that 'God so loved the world'. God does not love the rebellious system, but rather He loves sinners who are enslaved within the system.

It is to the rebellious system of the world to which John refers, and this is made clear in the next verse where he gives us three categories of sinful behavior, that those enslaved within the world system, manifest in their lives. Here then is John's fifth mark of a Christian, a person who has overcome the world through the power of Christ.

16 *For everything in the world - the cravings of sinful man, the lust of his eyes, and the boasting of what he has and does - comes not from the Father but from the world.*

Cravings of Sinful Man

Craving is a strong word which denotes a form of slavery to something. Peter tells us that a man is a slave to whatever has mastered him (2nd Peter 2:19). Throughout our lives, before we are born again, we yield to the things we desire and crave until we become slaves to sin. Many people become addicted, both emotionally and physically, to various things which we perceive as necessary from a sinful and even natural perspective.

We are complex creatures. Our parents are often people who are struggling with habits and cravings which have manifested themselves because of their own upbringings, for both nature and nurture play an important role in our development.

For example, the person who grows up with little or no physical or verbal demonstrations of love may develop an emotional addiction to pornography, replacing through fantasy the love he craves. Rejection, bitterness, loneliness, sickness, and a multitude of other things, can shape the way we process information and, ultimately, determine how we relate and react to others. In essence, we form habits through craving for what we are convinced we lack.

The world also tells us that success is measured by material wealth, that poverty is failure, so many people neglect those things that money can't buy in their craving to be accepted. The world conditions us; its principals and standards are drummed into us through advertising, peer pressure and the like. We easily become slaves to whatever we crave and, if we continue to look to the world for satisfaction, we will never be free.

Also, many people become slaves to what they desire. 'If I never find and marry the right person, I will never be happy', 'if I cannot have children I will never be happy', 'if I never find a good job or get out of this little town, I will never be happy'. Whatever we believe is the source of our satisfaction and happiness, that thing or person is our idol and we its slave.

For the Christian, only Christ can be in that place, for only He and His plan for our lives can fully satisfy. Those who are in Christ are no longer slaves to the cravings of their sinful natures. Paul explains this well in Romans 6.

The Lust of our Eyes

The lust of the eyes is as old as temptation itself. Eve looked on the fruit that was forbidden and saw that it was 'pleasing to the eye' (Genesis 3:6). The word 'lust' means to earnestly desire something, usually in order to satisfy a longing. One of the Ten Commandments basically sums this up as 'do not covet'. Coveting is utterly opposed to God's will because it desires what we are often forbidden to have. Like the cravings of sinful man, the lust of the eyes looks at the material world for answers to dissatisfaction, and therefore, turns away from the Lord who promises to provide all we need.

The lust of the eyes is a far wider problem than the obvious ties to improper sexuality with which we often associate it. Many Christians seek temporary satisfaction in clothing, jewelry, the latest gadget, constantly renovating their home, gluttony, an excessive amount of vacations - the list goes on and on. The Scriptures warn about this problem because we are called to live in freedom from what this world promises. God wants us to know the joy of being satisfied. Paul wrote that *godliness with contentment is great gain (1st Timothy 6:6).*

Can you be content; are you content with what the Lord has given you? That is the essential question that every Christian must ask. The book of Job tells the story of a wealthy man who lost everything he cherished in this world. His wife advised him to curse God and die, but he chose to remain faithful saying 'the Lord gives and the Lord takes away; blessed be the name of the Lord'.

Like almost every aspect of our Christian life it is a matter of trust. Can you come to God every day with open hands? That is the heart of 'taking up our cross'. Are we willing to trust Him to place in our hands what He knows is best, and to take out what He no longer wants us to have? If we can, we will live a life free of coveting, content to let Christ be Lord.

Boasting of what we Have and Do

In Christians, boasting of what we *do* is often tied to our need for acceptance and worldly notions of success, but can also manifest itself in telling others of how we are serving Christ. We are brought up in a world of competition. In public schools we are engaged in tests, exams, sports and popularity contests, daily. The world teaches us to measure our success against other people and to strive to get awards and recognition for the highest grade, for being a sports star, for being the prettiest girl, smartest guy, etc. Competition becomes ingrained into all that we do and we may carry this habit of boasting into our new Christian life.

Paul tells us that we should test our own actions and not to compare ourselves with others (Galatians 6:4). Pride is one worldly vice which God hates, in fact,

71

the Scriptures tell us in several places that God 'actively opposes the proud, but gives grace to the humble'. Paul tells us to boast in the Lord. He doesn't mean to boast about our service to God, but to boast about what God has done for us as pathetic sinners. *If anyone thinks he is something when he is nothing, he deceives himself (Galatians 6:3)*, Paul says.

We mustn't compare ourselves with others. Be aware that we have been conditioned by the cultures in which we grew up. Be aware of our habit to compete, and be aware of the fundamental problem of human pride.

Material wealth can also be an area of boasting. For Christians in any culture, boasting in what we have is ungodly, unless our boast is that Christ in His mercy and grace has made us His heirs. The wealth and prosperity doctrine, which I believe is absolutely contrary to Scripture, tries to give Christians a Biblical mandate for greed. Not surprisingly then, the largest church congregation in the U.S. teaches that God wants you to have an abundant life, a term meaning that God wants you to be wealthy and prosperous in material things. I doubt that the leaders of such churches ever spend much time preaching 'blessed are the poor'.

Take the time to study your Bible and see if you can find a single verse where Jesus praises the idea of material wealth. Read 1st Timothy 6:3-10, stand back and take another look at prosperity theology. Jesus never had two coins to rub together. He taught a basic and incredibly important principal. Those who have everything in the material world will find it almost impossible to feel that they need God.

72

When Jesus sent out the disciples into the world He ordered them to take nothing with them. His purpose was to teach them two things. Firstly, to understand that we are aliens in this world; citizens of another place, and secondly, to live in this attitude and rely on God for all we need. This doesn't mean it is wrong to own a house, a car and to have enough for an annual vacation. It means that our hearts should always be focused on our true inheritance which is in Christ, and not on this world.

In verse 17 John summarizes.

17 The world and its desires pass away, but the man who does the will of God lives forever.

John's summary challenges us in several ways. Firstly, in asking the question 'what are we living for?' All of us are going to leave this world and enter into eternity. At that moment, for us, both the world and its desires will pass away. Will we stand before the Lord as people who lived with eternal values, people who invested our time and wealth into His kingdom, or as people who lived for the world's values?

Secondly, we must always keep in mind that we are *as aliens and strangers in the world (1st Peter 2:11),* a people who are sojourners, just passing through. Paul calls us citizens of heaven (Philippians 3:20), a people who no longer belong to this world, therefore, we should live as such, keeping our hearts and minds on things above.

Thirdly, John reminds us that this world will pass away, it is temporary and destined for destruction. Peter tells us about this destruction (2nd Peter 3:10-13) and asks the question 'what kind of people ought we to be?' Peter answers his own question (v11); that we should live holy and godly lives, and John reminds us that *the man who does the will of God lives forever.*

Study Eight

The Spirit of Antichrist

1st John 2:18-27, 4:1-6

18 Dear children, this is the last hour; and as you have heard that the antichrist is coming, even now many antichrists have come. This is how we know it is the last hour. 19 They went out from us, but they did not really belong to us. For if they had belonged to us, they would have remained with us; but their going showed that none of them belonged to us.

20 But you have an anointing from the Holy One, and all of you know the truth. 21 I do not write to you because you do not know the truth, but because you do know it and because no lie comes from the truth. 22 Who is the liar? It is the man who denies that Jesus is the Christ. Such a man is the antichrist - he denies the Father and the Son; whoever acknowledges the Son has the Father also. 23 No one who denies the Son has the Father: whoever acknowledges the Son has the Father.

24 See that what you have heard from the beginning remains in you. If it does, you also will remain in the Son and in the Father. 25 And this is what he promised us - even eternal life. 26 I am writing these things to you about those who are trying to lead you astray. 27 As for you, the anointing you received from him remains in you, and you do not need anyone to teach you. But as his anointing teaches you about all things and as that anointing is real, not counterfeit - just as it has taught you, remain in him.

In this section, and later in 4:1-6, John confronts the heresy of Docetism head-on. He also adds another mark of a true Christian, namely, that every true believer has received the Holy Spirit, that which he refers to as an *anointing*, which we will discuss in our next study. The evidence of the Holy Spirit's anointing is that true believers know the real nature of Jesus Christ. John leads into these topics with a statement about the last hour and antichrists, so we will work through these verses in their topical sequence.

(v18) John tells us that the *last hour* has come and that we know it is here because of the presence of antichrists. It is about 1,940 years since John wrote these words. Did he believe that the rise of the Antichrist figure and return of Jesus Christ were imminent events? Perhaps he did, indeed some suggest that he thought the Emperor Nero might be the antichrist he writes of in his Revelation.

We know that Paul (1st Corinthians 7:29), and perhaps Peter (2nd Peter 3), believed, at least for a time, that Jesus may return in their lifetimes. What is more important, however, is that John recognizes the presence of many antichrists as a sign that we are living in the last hour, or 'age' as it may also be translated.

John writes of both an Antichrist, a single person, and of antichrists. We can find a description of the Antichrist in 2nd Thessalonians 2:1-12, a person of extreme supernatural power who will perform *all kinds of counterfeit miracles, signs and wonders*. This person will claim to be the promised Messiah and his supernatural displays will be used to deceive the world of his claim.

76

But here John is more concerned about the antichrists who are trying to deceive those he refers to as his 'dear children'. These antichrists are heretics in the true sense of the word. A heretic is someone who claims to be Christian but teaches doctrines which deny the fundamental and non-negotiable claims of Christianity which John defines for us in the following verses.

John tells us (v19) that these heretics *went out from us*, they were people who previously shared fellowship with the true believers. Was their fellowship genuine? It appeared to be genuine, however, as we have seen in chapter one, there can be no true fellowship with those who are not truly born of God.

Remember that when the Spirit of God comes to dwell within us at new birth, we understand through Him the fundamental doctrines of His Divinity and humanity. So why does John label these people who 'went out from us' as antichrists? John gives two theological points which are non-negotiable Christian doctrines. Firstly, in 2:22.

22 Who is the liar? It is the man who denies that Jesus is the Christ. Such a man is the antichrist - he denies the Father and the Son; whoever acknowledges the Son has the Father also.

For John, anyone who denies that Jesus is the Christ is a liar, and anti-christ. This was the position of Israel's rulers, the Pharisees and Sadducees. As with those rulers, if anyone denies that Jesus is the Christ they are fundamentally saying that the Messiah is yet to come in the future, and therefore, will be amongst those who accept and embrace the false messiah who Paul defines as the Antichrist, the 'man of lawlessness' in 2nd Thessalonians.

The Old Testament prophecies about Christ, over 250 of them, and the evidence of Jesus' life, are more than enough to convince any who desire to know the truth, therefore, John calls them 'liars' who deny Jesus is the true Messiah.

John says that he writes because they *know the truth*. Here he is most likely referring to those who *went out from them* and later chose the position of denial. No doubt, while these ones were in the presence of John and other believers, they heard the truth of Christ in great detail, but he says that they *did not really belong to us*, they professed to believe but had not been born again, had not received the 'anointing' of the Holy Spirit. If they had been filled with the Holy Spirit they would have remained.

The second theological point John makes is found in 4:1-6 where the apostle again speaks of those who went out from the fellowship and promoted the *spirit of antichrist.* He writes the following;

4:1 Dear friends, do not believe every spirit, but test the spirits to see whether they are from God, because many false prophets have gone out into the world. 2 This is how you can recognize the Spirit of God: Every spirit that acknowledges that Jesus Christ has come in the flesh is from God, 3 but every spirit that does not acknowledge Jesus is not from God. This is the spirit of antichrist, which you have heard is coming and even now is already in the world.

4 You, dear children, are from God and have overcome them, because the one who is in you is greater than the one who is in the world. 5 They are from the world and therefore speak from the viewpoint of the world, and the world listens to them. 6 We are from God, and whoever knows God listens to us; but whoever is not from God does not listen to us. This is how we recognize the Spirit of truth and the spirit of falsehood.

Here we see John confronting the heresy of Docetism head-on. The Docetists claimed that Jesus had not 'come in the flesh', that He was not a real man with flesh and blood, but rather that He only appeared as such. The theological implications of this heresy are extremely serious. If Jesus was as the Docetists claimed, then no real sacrifice had been offered for sin, indeed, the cross was a deception and salvation is forfeit.

For the Docetists, and later Gnostics, all flesh was evil, therefore, they taught that there was no true incarnation or Jesus would have inherited this presumed evil. If we are to fully understand John's message we must first understand the New Testament meaning of the word 'flesh'.

In his gospel (1:14), John states that *the Word became flesh and lived for a while among us.* The word translated 'flesh' is the Greek *sarx.* This word is translated throughout the New Testament to mean both our physical bodies, and our sinful nature. There are those who teach that Jesus was not the natural son of His mother Mary because they believe that we are all 'born sinners'. Such people teach that Mary merely carried Jesus within her womb like a surrogate mother and was, therefore, not related to Him genetically at all.

A discussion about the characteristics of the fallen nature are beyond the scope of this study, however, it is important to understand that the idea of children born in sin was only introduced to Christian doctrine by Augustine of Hippo in the 4th century after Christ. Until Augustine introduced this idea, and the practice of infant baptism which followed from it, no Christian theologian taught that children were born sinners, but rather, became sinners through submitting to their autonomous natures and committing sin as stated in Romans 5:12.

The point of difference is simply this: to be born with a desire for autonomy is not the same as being born a sinner. Augustine taught that every person born had committed Adam's sin as if they were themselves in the Garden of Eden rebelling against God. Romans 5:12 is actually stating that death entered the world through one man's sin, and that death has come to all *because all sinned*. Sin itself cannot be inherited, because it is a conscious act of the will, whether against parents, who are in authority over their children, or against God independent of parents.

Others point to the idea that Jesus was the 'second Adam', however, if Jesus was not genetically related to His mother, then neither was he 'of the dust' as the first Adam and we are. The Roman Catholic Church invented the false teaching of an 'immaculate conception' to further distance the birth of Jesus from Augustine's view, when they realized that Mary's own blood had passed to the unborn Jesus through her umbilical cord.

The doctrine of the immaculate conception is the idea that Mary was supernaturally conceived without her parent's blood passing into her unborn body, and therefore, she was born perfect. This doctrine led to her being hailed as the 'Queen of Heaven' and worshipped as equal to God.

But John is not entering into a theological debate about the status of the fallen nature; such debates came in later centuries. John simply states the Word became 'flesh' (sarx), the exact same word used throughout the NT to refer to every person born of flesh and blood. The writer of Hebrews states the following:

14 Since the children have flesh and blood, he too shared in their humanity so that by his death he might destroy him who holds the power of death - that is, the devil - ...17 For this reason he had to be made like his brothers in every way, in order that he might become a merciful and faithful high priest in service to God, and that he might make atonement for the sins of the people (Hebrews 2:14-17).

This passage states categorically that Christ was like us *in every way*, sharing in our humanity, our flesh and blood. The passage also states the incredibly important reason that this must be so, in order to *make atonement for the sins of the people.*

As previously mentioned, if Jesus was not fully human, as we are human, then He could not make atonement for us, He cannot be our substitute, our sacrifice for sin. This is the issue that John is addressing in 4:1-6; this is what is at stake in the Docetist heresy that claimed Jesus was not 'flesh and blood', made like us in 'every way'.

When we understand what is at stake, we can better understand John's words in verses 20, and 26-27.

20 But you have an anointing from the Holy One, and all of you know the truth.

26 I am writing these things to you about those who are trying to lead you astray. 27 As for you, the anointing you received from him remains in you, and you do not need anyone to teach you. But as his anointing teaches you about all things and as that anointing is real, not counterfeit - just as it has taught you, remain in him.

It is the indwelling Holy Spirit who reveals the truth about the nature of Jesus Christ to us. John refers to this as an anointing which teaches us 'about all things'. Those he labels as antichrist denied the true nature of the Lord, proving that they had never received the anointing. If they had been true Christians, (a) they would have known the truth of Christ, and (b) have remained with the believers.

Summary

These days there is a great deal of speculation about the rise of the Antichrist figure both John and Paul warned us about. There are also differing views about the Great Tribulation of Revelation, the Rapture, and the role that Christians will play during the Last Days before the return of Jesus Christ and Great Judgment. My personal view is that speculation about whether or not the Antichrist has already been born is not where Christians should be focusing their attention.

Paul makes it very clear that the 'man of lawlessness' will have incredible supernatural powers, indeed, it is very likely that he will be able to imitate similar miracles which were performed by Jesus in order to deceive the world. If Christians are present in the world when he makes his appearance, he will be easily recognized by the miracles he performs.

John's intentions in writing about antichrists is not to tempt us into speculation, but to encourage us to stand on firm theology regarding the person and nature of Jesus Christ and the fact of His incarnation. In this regard we must reject any doctrine that denies the full Divinity and humanity of Jesus Christ or we have fallen to the heresy of the Docetists and Gnostics. Any who deny these non-negotiable truths prove that they do not possess the 'anointing', the indwelling Holy Spirit who has revealed the truth about Jesus Christ to us.

Study Nine

The Sixth Mark: Anointing of the Spirit

1st John 2:18-27, 4:1-6

18 Dear children, this is the last hour; and as you have heard that the antichrist is coming, even now many antichrists have come. This is how we know it is the last hour. 19 They went out from us, but they did not really belong to us. For if they had belonged to us, they would have remained with us; but their going showed that none of them belonged to us.

20 But you have an anointing from the Holy One, and all of you know the truth. 21 I do not write to you because you do not know the truth, but because you do know it and because no lie comes from the truth. 22 Who is the liar? It is the man who denies that Jesus is the Christ. Such a man is the antichrist - he denies the Father and the Son; whoever acknowledges the Son has the Father also. 23 No one who denies the Son has the Father; whoever acknowledges the Son has the Father also.

24 See that what you have heard from the beginning remains in you. If it does, you also will remain in the Son and in the Father. 25 And this is what he promised us - even eternal life. 26 I am writing these things to you about those who are trying to lead you astray. 27 As for you, the anointing you received from him remains in you, and you do not need anyone to teach you. But as his anointing teaches you about all things and as that anointing is real, not counterfeit - just as it has taught you, remain in him.

In our previous study we examined the link between false doctrines and those John considers antichrist. In this study we will consider John's claim that those who have the anointing of the Spirit 'know the truth'. What truth is John referring to? Primarily, he is telling us that those who have received the nature of Christ within, who have become partakers of the Holy Spirit, these ones will know the true nature of Jesus Christ.

In this context he writes that *no lie comes from the truth. Who is the liar? It is the man who denies that Jesus is the Christ. Such a man is the antichrist - he denies the Father and the Son; whoever acknowledges the Son has the Father also. No one who denies the Son has the Father; whoever acknowledges the Son has the Father also.*

When John writes of Jesus being the Christ, and the acknowledgment of the Son and Father, he is claiming that Jesus Christ is God in the flesh. In his gospel he opens by referring to Christ as the Logos, a passage we referred to in study one.

1. In the beginning was the Word, and the Word was with God and the Word was God. 2 He was with God in the beginning. 3 Through him all things were made; without him nothing was made that has been made. (John 1:1-3)

The Word became flesh and dwelt for a while among us. We have seen His glory, the glory of the one and only Son, who came from the Father, full of grace and truth. (John 1:14)

Firstly, in these few short verses John has told us that the pre-incarnate Christ (The Logos) was there in the beginning of creation. The Word (Logos) is with God and is God, indeed in the original Greek text the last part of verse one reads 'God was the Word'. The Logos is God the Son who is uncreated, He who has dwelt with the Father and Holy Spirit eternally.

Secondly, John echoes the first verse of Scripture which states that 'In beginning God created the heavens and the earth' (Genesis 1:1). It is the Logos, the Son, who is Creator of all things, for He is the *radiance of God's glory and the exact representation (manifestation) of his being, sustaining all things by his powerful word (Hebrews 1:3).*

Thirdly, it is this same Logos who *became flesh and dwelt for a while among us. We have seen His glory, the glory of the one and only Son, who came from the Father, full of grace and truth (John 1:14).* These are the truths that John is speaking of in the passage we are studying. It is through our being joined to Christ that these truths are revealed, that union which John calls the 'anointing from the Holy One'.

Having said that, in the last century the term 'anointing' has come to mean many things other than what John intended. Some claim that the anointing is a separate experience from being born again, that it is a special outpouring of the Holy Spirit *upon* (rather than within) particular believers.

In a similar way, it is claimed that John is referring to the Baptism of the Holy Spirit, and that this too, is a separate experience to new birth which empowers believers in spiritual/supernatural gifts. Such teachers claim that the disciples were 'Christians' before the day of Pentecost, and therefore, were not born again at Pentecost, but rather, being people who believed in Christ's resurrection, were automatically born again, and at Pentecost, empowered to Christian service.

If we believe the disciples were born again before Pentecost, then we will understand Pentecost as a mysterious 'second blessing' which should be accompanied by signs and wonders, such as speaking in tongues. We will also believe that there are two levels of Christians, those who have received the Spirit at conversion, but have no spiritual power, and those who have received what we label as a separate 'Baptism of the Spirit' and can manifest supernatural gifts.

There are many issues at stake here, and in order to correctly understand John's term 'anointing', it will be necessary to, at least briefly, examine each of them.

Were the disciples born again before Pentecost?

In John 14, Jesus, knowing that His arrest and crucifixion are imminent, comforts His disciples, preparing them for what is about to happen. From verse 15ff Jesus speaks about the Holy Spirit, calling Him 'another Counselor' to be with them forever. He explains in verse 17 that this 'Spirit of Truth' is *with* them and will be *in* them. Here we see a classic example between the old and new covenants. Under the old, the Holy Spirit was *upon* certain individuals, such as kings and prophets within the Old Testament. The new covenant is the Spirit within us. Jesus explains this in verse 23.

Jesus replied, 'If anyone loves me, he will obey my teaching. My Father will love him, and we will come to him and make our home with him'.

Later, in chapter 16, which is the same discourse from chapter 14, Jesus explains the work of the Holy Spirit. Again, He calls Him the 'Spirit of Truth', and promises to send Him to the disciples *after He has returned to the Father (16:5-11).* Jesus tells them that: *But I tell you the truth: It is good that I am going away. Unless I go away, the Counselor will not come to you (16:7).* Jesus is stating here that the Holy Spirit will only be sent to the disciples after He has returned to the Father.

We now move over to chapter 20 of John's gospel. The crucifixion has occurred, and John tells us of the events which happened up and until the time when Jesus returned to the Father. In verse 17, Jesus again speaks of His returning to the Father, and we are told (v19) that the disciples are hiding in a locked room *for fear of the Jews.*

In verse 20 Jesus appears to the frightened disciples and shows them His hands and side. There are only 10 of the disciples at this meeting, for Judas Iscariot is dead, and Thomas is away (v24). During this meeting (verses 21-23) we have this seemingly mysterious impartation of the Holy Spirit, which many (especially Pentecostals) claim to be the moment the disciples were born again before Pentecost.

21 Again Jesus said, 'Peace be with you! As the Father has sent me, I am sending you. 22 And with that

he breathed on them and said, 'Receive the Holy Spirit.
23 If you forgive anyone his sins, they are forgiven; if you
do not forgive them, they are not forgiven.'

Was this the moment the disciples were born again?
My answer to that question is an emphatic 'no'! Consider
the following:

1. There were 120 people in the upper room on the
Day of Pentecost (Acts 1:15), but only 10 of those
present had been with Jesus when He said 'receive the
Holy Spirit' in the passage we are examining. Therefore,
110 of them, including Thomas, had no prior impartation
before Pentecost, if we believe that any of them did.

2. In verse 21, Jesus is speaking of sending them as
the Father sent Him, and then in verse 22 we have the
'receive the Holy Spirit' commandment. We know from
the next chapter that His disciples returned to Galilee
and their old lives of fishing. Jesus appeared to them at
Galilee and re-instated Peter. Are we to believe that
Jesus imparted the Holy Spirit to them and then sent
them back to Galilee to take up their old lives as
commercial fishermen? We are told in Acts 1 that in fact
Jesus commanded them to return to Jerusalem and await
the promised Holy Spirit.

3. The passage we are studying actually gives us the
entire answer. As those who understand Greek have
noticed, the entire spoken words of Jesus in verses 21-23
are in the aorist tense, which means to receive something
once and for all time. However, what many miss is that
there are two aorist tenses, and the aorist 2 tense (which
is rare), is concerned with the future.

The entire passage is in the aorist 2 tense (future), and also in the imperative mood, which means that Jesus was giving a commandment. In other words, He was commanding them to receive the Holy Spirit, once and for all time, at a specific time in the future, namely, the Day of Pentecost. Also, the Greek word 'emphusao', translated as 'breathed on them', can simply mean 'breathed in', in fact the word to 'implant' something is a variant of this word, 'emphutos', and this word is not used.

4. Jesus had already told them that unless He goes to the Father, the Holy Spirit will not come to them. We know that His return happened after His re-instating Peter, and obviously after the passage in question, therefore, the Holy Spirit had not yet been sent to them.

5. Apart from the above, Peter makes it clear in his first sermon in Acts 2, that Pentecost was the fulfillment of Joel's prophecy about the outpouring of the Holy Spirit, and therefore, the inauguration of the New Covenant. Consider also the conversion of Cornelius and those in his household in Acts 10. Peter states that, *'Can anyone keep these people from being baptized with water? They have received the Holy Spirit just as we have'.* Peter is referring to what happened at Pentecost, not an imaginary impartation prior to Pentecost.

What then is the 'Baptism of the Holy Spirit' or 'Anointing'?

There is nothing in the New Testament to ever suggest that the Baptism of the Holy Spirit, or anointing, is a secondary experience to being born again. If this were the case we would have ample passages telling us to make sure we have had this 'second blessing', otherwise we would be powerless to live for Christ, and like Peter and the other disciples before Pentecost, would return to our old lives.

Paul tells us that *we were all baptized by one Spirit into one body (1 Corinthians 12:13).* Throughout his letters Paul confirms that the baptism of the Holy Spirit is the initial event of a person being born again, the moment that the Spirit of Truth takes up residence within them. Passages like Romans 8, Galatians 5, and many others, confirm this fundamental biblical truth.

However, there is a great deal of confusion, even amongst evangelicals, about when this event has occurred. Many use the book of Acts as a template for evangelism, and in my opinion this is foolish. The testimonies of people in Acts never follow some simple template for salvation, for this was a transitional period. Also, in Acts, we read of people from very different ethnic and cultural perspectives compared to modern day cultures.

For example, for both Jews and Gentile pagans in the 1st century, sacrifice to God, or Roman 'gods' was an everyday experience. These people all understood sacrifice as a necessary part of life, and for many, the consequences of following Christ were fatal. People were forced to count the cost (Luke 14) of becoming a Christian, therefore, their commitment was to 'deny self, take up their cross, and follow', even if that meant being dragged into a Roman arena to die, or crucified for refusing to pay homage to Roman gods.

When persecution ended in the 4th century, and Christianity joined the Roman Empire, Christianity became an intellectual assent to the Pope's demands, and cases of people having a born again experience are rare until the Reformation, some 1000 years later. But sadly, Jesus' command to count the cost (Luke 14) is extremely neglected today, and there are a great number of professing Christians who have said a 'sinner's prayer', but live as if they have no love of Christ, or desire to obey His commands.

Some of these eventually come to a crisis in their lives and truly repent, surrendering their lives to Christ, are filled with the Holy Spirit for the first time, and then go on to live obedient and holy lives. Some are told that this was their 'second blessing', but the truth is they were never born again until this moment.

'Under the Anointing'

Back in 2000 I was invited to a healing meeting by a group of theological students from Otago University in Dunedin, New Zealand. The meeting had been advertised on campus, heralding an American missionary who claimed to have raised the dead, healed hundreds and even have bullets pass through his body, all under the anointing of the Holy Spirit.

The speaker also claimed that he could prophesy with the same authority as the New Testament apostles. Reluctantly, I agreed to go. There were approximately 400 people in attendance, mostly Pentecostal Christians who had brought loved ones with various ailments, including cancer, and others who were crippled and in wheel-chairs.

After a series of songs the speaker gave us a one hour talk about his supernatural exploits while serving as a missionary in a South American country. He spoke constantly about the Holy Spirit coming upon him, and near the end of this talk, suddenly staggered across the stage, walking unsteadily as he said, "I love it when the spirit comes upon me". He then claimed that the Holy Spirit had told him to declare a promise, that every person in that meeting would be completely healed before they left to go home.

From then onwards, the meeting became extremely bizarre. A ten year old boy was brought to the stage and introduced as living evidence of someone the speaker had raised from death. The crowd clapped and shouted 'hallelujah', and 'amen', and the boy went back to his place.

The speaker then produced a large red handkerchief from his pocket, which he claimed was also anointed, and promised that whoever he touched with this item would be instantly healed, in the same way as those who touched items which had been in contact with the Apostle Paul in Acts 19:11-12.

He ordered people to line up according to their illnesses, and within minutes the aisles leading to the stage were full of expectant and convinced believers. There was a line of cancer sufferers, a line of those in wheel-chairs and lines for those with nonspecific diseases. He then proceeded to go from line to line waving his handkerchief, staggering under the 'anointing' and claiming that each and every person was completely healed.

When those being touched continued standing, he lay his hands on them and most fell to the floor where they remained, shaking, convulsing, moaning or laughing, all to the cries of hallelujah from onlookers, some of whom were yelling repeated lines of indiscernible gibberish.

My close friends and I all felt a presence which I can only describe as evil, and we decided to leave. Because the exits were blocked with people on the ground, we took the stairs to a lower floor where we passed another room which had been prepared for latecomers. There was a large TV screen showing, live, the activities going on up-stairs, provided for by several cameras. We paused and watched for another hour until the meeting was declared a huge success and people started to go home.

A few days later I met with the theology students who had attended the meeting, some who had brought their sick relatives. They were all very excited about what they had witnessed, sharing about how many people had fallen to the ground, and that they had rarely seen such a powerful anointing of the Spirit. I asked them some simple questions.

"Do any of you know of a single person who was healed at the meeting?"

"Lots of them", one man said, "there were literally dozens of people on the floor."

"But do you know of a single person who was healed of their illness, a single cancer patient, a single person who arrived in a wheel-chair and left walking?" I asked again.

There was silence, and then all of them admitted that, although they knew most of those who attended, there wasn't one single person who had been miraculously healed that they knew of.

"So tell me, then. Which one is the liar? The man who claimed that the Holy Spirit told him that every person he touched would be instantly and completely healed, or the 'spirit' he claims told him to say this?"

They were silent.

"Do you believe that the Holy Spirit could tell a lie?"

"No, of course not," they replied.

"Do you believe that those people, including some of you, were knocked to the ground by a supernatural force, a 'spirit' of some kind?"

"Yes".

"The same spirit that spoke through the speaker and claimed that not a single person would leave unhealed," I asked.

This question shook them to the core as they began to realize the implications. If the same spirit that knocked them to the ground had spoken a promise to heal all, then that spirit was a liar and deceiver. According to the speaker, it was the same spirit who had raised the dead, allowed bullets to pass through him, and heal thousands, the same spirit who suddenly 'came upon' him in such force he couldn't walk steadily for several minutes.

Yet not a single person left that place healed. Those who came in wheelchairs, left in wheelchairs, and even after weeks had gone by, not a single person claimed to have been cured of cancer or other serious disease.

Was this an anointing of the Holy Spirit? The answer to that question should be obvious, but more importantly, was John ever writing of the anointing as we hear it spoken of in such meetings today? Again, the answer is 'no'. John describes the anointing that all Christians have in these words.

26 I am writing these things to you about those who are trying to lead you astray. 27 As for you, the anointing you received remains in you, and you do not need anyone to teach you. But as his anointing teaches you about all things and as that anointing is real, not counterfeit - just as it has taught you, remain in him (1st John 2:26-27).

There are two points to notice here.

1. The anointing they received remains *in* them. John is never speaking of some spirit which must be invited to a meeting, a spirit which falls upon people in order to produce supernatural manifestations. The Holy Spirit *is* the anointing; He is within them and remains within them. As we have seen in our previous studies, it is the presence of the Divine Nature within us who teaches us, transforms us, gives us the power to obey and walk as Jesus walked. He never needs to be ushered into a meeting, or commanded to fall upon us, because He entered the meeting when those who are born again entered the meeting. We who are in Christ are God's house, His dwelling place, and He is where we are.

2. The anointing we have received, the Holy Spirit, is *real - not counterfeit.* John recognizes the reality of a counterfeit anointing. A counterfeit is something which appears to be the real thing, but is in reality a fake. This is why John warns them about *those who are trying to lead them astray.* Satan is the master counterfeiter, the one who tries in every way to lead us astray, deceive us, and destroy our relationship with Christ through false teachings and practices.

Summary

There is a great deal more we could discuss in regards to the anointing of the Spirit, especially concerning the practices and claims of various Pentecostal and Charismatic groups. I have often heard from these groups' leaders that supernatural manifestations are not occurring in non-charismatic circles because of a lack of faith. On the contrary, my view is that a lust and hunger for signs and wonders may be far greater evidence of a lack of faith, or a lack of the real anointing which dwells within. Jesus Himself said that *it is a wicked and adulterous generation that demand a sign (Matthew 12:39)*, in response to the Pharisees wanting proof of who He was.

When I hear people claiming that their gift of tongues is evidence that they are born again, and that so-called gift is one line of indiscernible gibberish they babble repeatedly, I long for such people to be born again. Those who know Christ need no external proofs of their relationship, for *the Spirit Himself testifies with our spirit that we are children of God* (Romans 8:16, Galatians 4:6).

I believe that the gifts of the Holy Spirit are available to Christians in this day and age, but only as the Lord directs, for His purpose, and in His will. Yet when I hear claims of gold flakes and feathers falling from the ceiling, and watch people crawling about on their hands and knees squealing like animals, or laughing as if drunk, totally out of control, convulsing etc, I am reminded of the demonic New Age meetings I attended, before being born again, where such manifestations occurred frequently.

97

In such cases, I am convinced that this is what John calls a 'counterfeit anointing', manifestations which have their roots in the demonic, and my heart grieves for those involved in such practices.

Christianity is both event and process. The event is the Baptism of the Spirit which occurs when we are born again, that moment when we become partakers of the Divine Nature, and the process is the ongoing proof of regeneration which is seen in the transformation of our lives through the fruits of the Holy Spirit being produced by His holy influence.

Paul commands us to be continually filled with the Holy Spirit (Ephesians 5:17), that which occurs through prayer and obedience to living for Christ, and in the knowledge that through His indwelling presence, we have an anointing from the Holy One who remains in us.

Study Ten

The Seventh Mark: Abiding in Him

1st John 2:28 - 3:3

28 And now, dear children, continue in him, so that when he appears we may be confident and unashamed before him at his coming. 29 If you know that he is righteous, you know that everyone who does what is right has been born of him.

In this section John addresses his readers with a word, 'children' (Gk. *teknia*) which denotes close family relationships. Also, the NIV translates the Greek *meno* as 'continue' in him, but the context is closer to other translations which use 'abide'. These two words have subtle differences in meaning in modern usage. The word abide expresses the idea of walking closely in relationship, whereas 'continue' has a less intimate meaning. John's appeal has a strong emotional element which is seen in the latter part of the sentence where he speaks of confidence and shame, and in the first verses of chapter three where he writes of the love that the Father has lavished upon us.

John is telling us to abide, and continue abiding in Christ, to stay close and in intimate fellowship with Him, otherwise, we will have no confidence when He appears, but rather feel shame that we have neglected our relationship with Him. But there is another element of warning here which is expressed in the word 'confidence'; something John has previously alluded to in 2:19 when he writes of those who *went out from us* and *did not belong to us.*

For John, abiding in Christ is one of the marks of a true Christian, for abiding also means to 'remain'. Only those who continually abide and remain in Christ can have confidence that they belong to Christ, and to the Body of Christ, therefore, it is essential that we understand what it means to abide.

What does it mean to 'abide in Christ'?

In order to answer this question we turn to John's gospel, chapter 15, where Jesus uses this word *meno* (abide, remain, continue) many times in His teaching on the Vine and the branches.

1 "I am the true vine and my Father is the gardener. 2 He cuts off every branch in me that bears no fruit, while every branch that does bear fruit he trims clean so that it will be even more fruitful. 3 You are already clean because of the word I have spoken to you. 4 Remain in me, and I will remain in you. No branch can bear fruit by itself; it must remain in the vine. Neither can you bear fruit unless you remain in me.

5 "I am the vine; you are the branches. If a man remains in me and I in him, he will bear much fruit; apart from me you can do nothing. 6 If anyone does not remain in me, he is like a branch that is thrown away and withers; such branches are picked up, thrown into the fire, and burned. 7 If you remain in me and my words remain in you, ask whatever you wish, and it will be given to you. 8 This is to my Father's glory, that you bear much fruit, showing yourselves to be my disciples."

Firstly, it is important to remember that this teaching of Jesus' has a future component. He has just finished telling His disciples that He must go away (John 14:1-4) and that He will send the Holy Spirit to them and be within them (14:15-20). This is fulfilled when He ascends to the Father after His resurrection and the Holy Spirit comes to inaugurate the new covenant on the Day of Pentecost. With that in mind let us examine several points about abiding.

Abiding means Union with Christ

To be in the Vine is to be united with Christ. This is the internal connection we receive when the Divine Nature comes to take residence within us. His life, joy, love, power and peace flow into us as a vine feeding the branches. This is the new life we begin at our new birth, the life-giving and life-changing nature of God who gives us the faith to trust in Him in every aspect of our lives. Jesus tells them;

4 Remain in me and I will remain in you, and 6 If anyone does not remain in me, he is like a branch that is thrown away and withers; such branches are picked up, thrown into the fire, and burned.

There are those who believe that these verses teach that a person can be in Christ, and then out of Christ and lose their salvation. Firstly, remembering the future element of this teaching, and that *memo* means abide and remain, we have a clear understanding. If we abide in Christ, He abides in us. If anyone does not abide in

Christ, Christ does not abide in Him, and is *like a branch* that is thrown away, withers, is picked up, thrown into the fire and burned. Those who take these verses to suggest that one can lose their salvation, have to assume that the person was actually joined to the Vine, and cut off. But the analogy simply says they were 'like' a branch that is thrown away.

Judas Iscariot heard this teaching of Jesus, but he never made it to Pentecost, he was never born again, he never experienced what it means to abide in Christ or have Him abide in us. In John's opinion, any person who appeared to be abiding, 'like' a true Christian, but did not remain, was never abiding in the first place, as we saw in study six.

They went out from us, but they did not really belong to us. For if they had belonged to us, they would have remained with us; but their going showed that none of them belonged to us (1 John 2:19).

But the key to understanding these verses is in the fact that by our fruits we are known to be in Christ or not, as Jesus warned in Matthew 7:15-23 where He speaks of false Christians who claimed to act in His name, but never knew Him.

Abiding means Fruitfulness

Being in the Vine means that through our internal union we will bear the fruit of the Vine. That fruit is the fruit of the Spirit; love, joy, peace, patience, kindness, goodness, faithfulness, gentleness, self-control, perseverance, endurance and godliness (Galatians 5:22-

23, 2nd Peter 1:5-7). If we are not truly in the Vine then we will not produce the fruit of the Vine, for, as Jesus said;

4 "Remain in me, and I will remain in you. No branch can bear fruit by itself; it must remain in the vine. Neither can you bear fruit unless you remain in me.

5 I am the vine; you are the branches. If a man remains in me and I in him, he will bear much fruit; apart from me you can do nothing."

If a person, who claims to be a Christian, is not producing the fruit of the Spirit, then that person's Christianity is merely outward and artificial. If the essence of the Vine is flowing into us, then spiritual fruit is inevitable, not optional. The fruit we produce is solely as a result of being united to the Vine, and in this we glorify the Father and prove we are Jesus' disciples as he said:

8 This is to my Father's glory, that you bear much fruit, showing yourselves to be my disciples."

Abiding means Pruning

Abiding in the Vine is the internal union we have in Christ, but Jesus also tells us that the Father is a gardener (or vinedresser) who continually cuts off the parts which are unclean in order that we might be *even more fruitful.* Peter speaks of the fruits of the Spirit as qualities we must possess in *increasing measure (2nd Peter 1:8),* and the writer to the Hebrews tells us that God, our Father;

103

... disciplines us for our good, that we may share in his holiness. No discipline seems pleasant at the time, but painful. Later on, however, it produces a harvest of righteousness and peace for those who have been trained by it (Hebrews 12:10-11).

Whilst Christ feeds our souls internally, the Father prunes us externally so that we might produce a harvest of righteousness as we submit to His discipline in our lives. Those who refuse to submit to this discipline are considered to be *illegitimate children and not true sons (Hebrews 11:8).*

Abiding means Confidence without Shame

28 And now, dear children, continue in him, so that when he appears we may be confident and unashamed before him at his coming.

As we continually abide in Christ we will be ready to meet Him face to face, either when we part from this world through death, or at His second coming. Notice that John includes himself (we) in his warning; *we may have confidence.* John was there in the Garden of Gethsemane when Jesus was arrested...he fled. John was with Peter and ran to the tomb to find it empty, and when Mary Magdalene came to the disciples and testified to our Lord's resurrection, he, and all of them, doubted her (Mark 16:11-12).

When the resurrected Christ appeared before them after Mary's proclamation, did John and his fellow-disciples feel ashamed? I have no doubts that they did.

John challenges us to be sure that we are ready to see Him face to face when He returns.

Christians are often ridiculed for our belief in the return of Jesus Christ. 1st century Christians faced similar ridicule (2nd Peter 3:3). John wants to encourage us to hold onto the hope that we have. He has just finished speaking of the anointing we share in the Holy Spirit, and here he reminds us to abide in that relationship. As we abide with Christ our confidence remains firm, and when we and the entire world witness His glorious return, we will not be ashamed. Perhaps John also has Jesus' words of warning from Mark 8:38 in mind, where the Lord tells us;

If anyone is ashamed of me and my words in this adulterous generation, the Son of Man will be ashamed of him when he comes in his Father's glory with the holy angels.

Summary

Abiding in Christ is one of the marks of a true Christian. This word means to be united, to remain and to continue in Christ. The apostle Paul teaches something very similar in Colossians 1:23 where he states that we are reconciled to Christ, and then adds a condition;

...if you continue in your faith, established and firm, not moved from the hope held out in the gospel.

Those who are truly in Christ, continue in Christ, they are unmoved from the hope they have, they remain in the place of abiding. We live as the Children of God, His life flowing through and within us, and His Fatherly discipline trimming and cleaning us in our flesh nature so that we produce a harvest of righteousness, the fruit of the Spirit in increasing measure.

Let us make every effort to submit to His loving discipline so that we may daily know the joy of walking closely with Him, and be unashamed when we see Him face to face.

Study Eleven

The Eighth Mark: Children of God

1st John 3:1-3

3:1 How great is the love the Father has lavished on us, that we should be called the children of God! And that is what we are! The reason the world does not know us is that it did not know him. 2 Dear friends, now we are children of God, and what we will be has not yet been made known. But we know that when he appears, we shall be like him, for we shall see him as he is. 3 Everyone who has this hope in him purifies himself, just as he is pure.

Throughout his letter John continually encourages and challenges us as to how we should live for Christ. He has presented many marks of a true Christian disciple, not so that we should be hunting through the congregation to find the 'goats', but always to remind us to examine ourselves, to ask ourselves if we are walking as Jesus walked. We may also have noticed that he constantly makes references to the second coming of Christ and the end of this age of worldly rebellion (1:8, 2:17, 2:18, 2:28).

The passage above is no exception, for both themes, the return of Christ and our living in purity, are mentioned. John has just finished warning us about loving the world, the anointing we have in Christ, and abiding in the Lord, and now his thoughts turn to the

One who has made all this possible, the One who calls us His children.

He begins with the word 'look', or 'behold' (Gk. *horao*) which is paraphrased as 'how great' in the NIV, a word he uses to make an exclamation somewhat similar to the modern use of 'wow'. John is expressing a powerful emotion here, he is saying 'how amazing and incredible is *the love the Father has lavished on us, that we should be called the children of God'*.

And not only are we called His children, he continues, but *that is what we are.* God has indeed made us to be what He has called us to be, therefore, we should have no doubts about who and what we are. There are many Christians who have failed to grasp the depth of John's statement, or the exclusivity he is claiming, so we will begin with examining the way the world views this topic.

The World's View

It is common to hear politicians and world leaders, whilst making statements about religious differences, tolerance etc, say 'we are all God's children'. The idea expressed here is well known; God created the world, He created mankind, therefore we are all God's creation/children whether we know Him or not, or however we perceive God to be. This is the heart of pluralism, the idea that all religions are of equal value, and none can be exclusively called the children of God because we are all His creations. The ideology of pluralism is intended to encourage tolerance and acceptance of all humanity as equal in the eyes of God, even if some of those included consider themselves atheists.

Universalism takes pluralism one step further. This is the view that because we are all God's children, all will eventually be saved, either in this life or the next, even the atheist. Universalists believe that a loving God with foreknowledge would never have begun the creation of humanity without the intention of saving them all.

Several Scriptures are cited to support this view such as in Malachi 2:10 which asks, *have we not all one Father? Did not one God create us?* In context, this verse is addressed to the Levitical priests who have broken their covenant with the Lord, and the prophet goes on to offer warnings which have eternal consequences.

Likewise, Universalists quote New Testament verses out of context to support their claims, even when the verses immediately before and following contradict them. A classic example is John 3:17: *For God did not send his Son into the world to condemn the world , but to save the world through him.*

Although the previous well-known verse makes a distinction of those who believe having eternal life rather than perishing, and the next verse (18) says that non-believers are condemned already, universalists simply ignore those passages which contradict their agenda.

Verses which use the word 'all' are especially cited (e.g. 2 Corinthians 5:14), but always out of context. In order to be a universalist, one must ignore or remove the vast amount of warnings within Scripture about judgment, hell, and the consequences of rejecting salvation in Christ.

The Biblical View

The Biblical view contradicts pluralism and universalism entirely. Yes, God is the Creator of all, however, He has endowed His creations with a free will and given us a measure of independence. Like hyper-Calvinism, universalism basically denies a person's freedom to obey or reject God's command to believe. Both doctrines teach a form of predestination which completely contradicts free-will; in hyper-Calvinism, only those predetermined will be saved, and in universalism everyone will be saved whether they wish it or not.

In one sense, all people are reliant on God, even for the breath in their lungs, yet He has given us the freedom to reject His call, to even deny His existence and hold on to our cherished autonomy. Such people are referred to in Scripture as enemies of God (Romans 5:10, Colossians 1:21), and even children of their father the devil (John 8:44).

The Bible makes a clear distinction between the children of the world, those who align themselves with the 'god of this world' (2 Corinthians 4:4), Satan, and the children of God. The biblical view is basically divided into two parts which are associated with the old and new covenants. We will examine each one separately.

Old Covenant Children (Sons of God)

The nation of Israel traces its lineage back to the person of Abraham. In Exodus 4:22 God refers to Israel as His 'first born son', and warns Pharaoh that if he refuses to let Israel leave Egypt, then the firstborn of Egypt will die. The concept of the first born relates especially to certain privileges and inheritance. Israel is the chosen nation, a nation chosen to reveal God to the world, chosen to be separate from the pagan nations around them, and chosen as the nation through whom God would enter this world in the person of Jesus Christ. Israel is also the nation of inheritance, especially concerning the land which God promised to them as descendents of the patriarch Abraham.

As a nation, Israel, under the old covenant, is connected to God through the person of Abraham, therefore, they are often referred to as children of Abraham, Isaac and Jacob, the latter whose name was changed to Israel. In this sense, they are not children of God from an eternal or spiritual perspective, but more so through their human heritage and the land. This connection is seen in Jeremiah 3:19 where the Lord says;

"...How gladly would I treat you as sons and give you a desirable land, the most beautiful inheritance of any nation. I thought you would call me 'Father' and not turn away from following me."

In this passage the word 'sons' is used as an analogy, but more importantly, it expresses the kind of relationship God wants to have with us, a relationship which was fundamentally impossible under the Old Covenant, as we shall discover.

The apostle Paul also makes an important distinction between the children of Abraham and what he calls the 'children of the promise' in Romans 9. In verse 4 Paul says that the people of Israel are adopted as sons, but this is in reference to their human ancestry from Abraham (v 5). He goes on to write that not all who are Abraham's descendents are Abraham's children, only those who are included in the promises made to Abraham, promises concerning salvation.

Therefore, in respect to the Jews under the Old Covenant, those, who like Abraham lived by faith before the Law, and like Moses, David and others after the Law, such are rightfully children of God through faith, for the true children of God are those who are saved.

God also uses other relationship types as analogies throughout the Old Testament such as Israel as an adulterous wife and prostitute (Jeremiah 3:6-9), but nearly always in the context that God Himself is the only faithful one in the relationship.

In general terms, then, the relationship types used under the Old Covenant, between God and Israel, are analogies which point towards the New Covenant, for only with a complete change of heart through new birth could these analogies become reality.

We should also note, that in the Old Testament, one of the main uses of the term 'sons of God' is referring to the angels, such as in Genesis 6:2,4 and Job 1:6, 2:1, 38:7.

New Covenant Children (Sons of God)

The essential doctrine of the New Covenant, concerning the children of God, is in the difference between the natural and the spiritual, the spirit and the flesh. Abraham, Moses and David, along with others, and those listed in Hebrews 11, were never born of the Spirit, for they all lived before the New Covenant was inaugurated on the Day of Pentecost. They are children of God through faith in what was to come, as Hebrews 11:39-40 states;

These were all commended for their faith, yet none of them received what had been promised. 40 God had planned something better for us so that only together with us would they be made perfect.

These Old Testament saints were 'saved', but not 'born again', the Spirit of God was upon them, but not dwelling permanently within them, for a perfect sacrifice for sin had to be accomplished before human beings could become the temple of the living God. Yet, like the Old Testament saints, it is only through faith that we can enter into a 'Father/child' relationship with God.

When we surrender our lives to Christ through faith in Him our former connection with the world is broken, and we are reborn into a new family, God's family. This is the spiritual reality of dying with Christ. The 'old self' is crucified with Christ and the new person becomes a child of God through being united with Christ (Romans 6).

How can we know that this death and rebirth has occurred? Paul explains this beautifully in Romans 8: 14-16.

...14 because those who are led by the Spirit of God are sons of God. 15 For you did not receive a spirit that makes you a slave again to fear, but you received the Spirit of sonship. And by him we cry, "Abba, Father." 16 The Spirit himself testifies with our spirit that we are God's children.

In the text we are studying John makes the same claim as Paul but in a different way. *The reason the world does not know us is that it did not know him.* When we were of the world, the world knew us and what we were, for we were of the same family of rebellion. But now that we know Jesus Christ we belong to a heavenly family and the world no longer recognizes us.

Exclusivity

There are several verses which declare the exclusivity of those who are God's children. These verses point out the differences between those who are in Christ and those who are not. In the following examples Paul compares God's children with a crooked and depraved generation, and John with those who are under the control of Satan.

...it is God who works in you to will and to act according to his good purpose. 14 Do everything without complaining or arguing, 15 so that you may become

114

blameless and pure, children of God without fault in a crooked and depraved generation, in which you shine like stars in the universe... (Philippians 2:13-15)

We know that we are children of God, and that the whole world is under the control of the evil one (1st John 5:19).

In John 1:11-13, the apostle tells us that the world did not recognize the Word, the *Logos*, even those who 'were his own', the Jews, rejected Him as their Messiah.

Yet to all who received him, to those who believed in his name, he gave the right to become children of God - 13 children born not of natural descent, nor of human decision or a husband's will, but born of God.

In this passage John stresses both the exclusive nature of being a child of God and God's initiative in making this happen. We cannot inherit the right to become God's children through natural descent (born a Jew or into a Christian family), nor be declared such by a human authority (husband's will), and neither do we have the authority to tell anyone that they are born of God (human decision).

It is He who reveals Himself, He who convicts of sin, He who calls, and He who decides when we are ready to surrender our wills to His will. Our part is to seek and obey Him when called, believe on His name and receive Him as Lord and Savior.

Yes, there is a human decision to reject or receive Him, but no person comes to that moment of decision unless the Lord Himself has brought them to that place.

Salvation is wholly the work of Christ, and even the faith to believe (which means to cast our whole weight upon), is a gift from God.

None of us can make ourselves 'born again', for none of us has the power to 'crucify our egos' (Colossians 2:20), or take up our cross and follow Him. It is all and always about Christ, our part is simply to obey His calling and receive His reward (Hebrews 11:6).

Summary and Conclusions

As Malachi 2:10 and Deuteronomy 32:6 state, in one sense we all have one Father, if we are speaking of God as our Creator and source of life. However, those John speaks of as children of God are His spiritual children, those who have undergone a second birth into His eternal spiritual family.

The difference between these two kinds of children is as black and white, natural and spiritual, life and death, for God's adopted children will live with Him forever, whilst those who have chosen to reject His grace and forgiveness, will be eternally separated from Him and all that He is. When a non-christian sins he sins against his Creator, but if a Christian sins, he sins against his Father.

John begins chapter three with a sense of awe. He recognizes that it is entirely through God's love and grace that we are called the children of God. Sadly, in this age in which we live there are those who claim to be Christians and speak as though they should pat themselves on the back for deciding to follow Christ, if indeed they are following at all.

Being a child of God draws our eyes to always gaze upon the cross of Christ. It is only in the cross that we see God's plan in bringing us into His eternal family. What an incredible display of love that Jesus Christ would offer Himself as a sacrifice for our sins so that we might belong to Him and be called His children. For this reason, John calls us to live pure lives which reflect the purity of our Lord and bring honor to our status as children of God.

Study Twelve

The Ninth Mark: The Root of Sin Destroyed

1st John 3:4-9

4 Everyone who sins breaks the law; in fact sin is lawlessness. 5 But you know that he appeared so that he might take away our sins. And in him is no sin. 6 No one who lives in him keeps on sinning. No one who continues to sin has either seen him or known him. 7 Dear children, do not let anyone lead you astray. He who does what is right is righteous, just as he is righteous.

8 He who does what is sinful is of the devil, because the devil has been sinning from the beginning. The reason the Son of God appeared was to destroy the devil's work. 9 No one who is born of God will continue to sin, because God's seed remains in him; he cannot go on sinning, because he has been born of God. 10 This is how we know who the children of God are and who the children of the devil are: Anyone who does not do what is right is not a child of God; neither is anyone who does not love his brother.

This passage of Scripture is often misunderstood and misinterpreted. There are currently three interpretations of what John is saying here, one of which is impossible, and two which are quite similar.

1. The first interpretation is to take an absolutely literal meaning without consulting other Scripture, even Scripture in the previous chapters of this letter of John's (1:8). Therefore, when we read John's repeated words

118

that those who are born again cannot continue to sin, this is taken to mean that any who claim to be Christian, and commit any form of sin, are simply not children of God, but children of the devil.

Surprisingly, there are Christians who teach that this is the correct interpretation of these verses, despite the fact that in 1:8 John tells Christians that to claim to be without sin is to deceive ourselves. Such people also say that in 1:8 John is speaking to non-Christians, however, this too is false as John calls his readers 'my dear children' just two verses later regarding the same topic.

There are Christians who believe that only sins which are acted out in the physical realm are meant by John, however, John never makes a distinction between physical sins such as adultery, fornication, murder etc, or sins such as envy, coveting, hatred and the like.

The question is simply this: do Christians sometimes sin? The answer, if a person is honest, is 'yes we do', indeed, John tells us in 1:10 that to claim that we have not sinned as Christians is to call Christ a liar, and the NT has many examples and warnings to Christians to refrain from all forms of sin. In short, this interpretation is absolutely wrong and should be rejected completely.

2. The second interpretation takes into account John's style of writing and supporting Scripture. The emphasis is on the fact of regeneration, of the indwelling Divine nature, and on being new creations and children of God. The argument goes like this. If a person is born again, the old person is dead and a new creation lives. The Divine nature within the believer cannot sin because God cannot sin.

The Christian has the same 'seed' as his Divine Parent. Galatians 2:20, and Romans 7 are cited to support this view. In the Galatians verse Paul says he has been crucified with Christ and no longer lives his own life, but rather it is Christ living within him. In Romans 7, it is presumed that Paul is speaking of before his new birth where he says that he does what he doesn't want to do (v 16) and it is no longer he that is doing it, but sin living in him. Therefore, this interpretation dissects a Christian into parts, old nature and new nature, flesh and soul.

Although this interpretation correctly portrays an extremely important part of John's teaching, it could be considered dangerous as it may be used to support a Gnostic view. A large percentage of Gnostics taught that nothing a person did in the body could affect the soul. This form of Gnosticism is seen in its infancy in Paul's letter to the Corinthians where sexual immorality was rampant in the Church.

In a similar way, our second interpretation, if taken to the extreme, may suggest a form of grace which divides the old and new natures within a Christian to a point where the person may think that sins committed cannot affect our fellowship with God.

3. The third interpretation is that John is speaking of the root of sin, the unregenerate rebellious nature which must be crucified with Christ. Notice firstly that John tells us that sin is lawlessness, it is breaking the law. We know that John is not claiming that Christians must keep the Mosaic Law, for this would completely contradict the entire teaching of Galatians. Rather, he is speaking of the root of sin which is rebellion against God, and for this reason, he mentions Satan as the one who was sinning from the beginning, long before the Mosaic Law existed.

Satan's sin was rebellion, a refusal to submit to God...this is the essence of lawlessness and the root of all sin (see Isaiah 14:12-15, Ezekiel 28:11-17). In these passages, Satan, the 'guardian cherub' (angel) became proud, he said in his heart he would 'raise his throne above the stars of God' and 'make himself like the Most High'. Satan desired to 'make himself', to become what *he* intended, to rule his own life.

As it is in Satan, this rebellion is also rooted in the sin nature, or self-ruling nature, the human ego. In Colossians 2:20, Paul says 'I' (ego) have been crucified with Christ. Our egos must be crucified, the rebellion ended, the desire to rule our own lives destroyed as we submit our wills to our Creator's will.

Satan, and all non-Christians, refuse to submit to God, but the Christian has submitted their will to God's will, and in this they are crucified with Christ, have taken up their cross. When a Christian sins, and we do, we are convicted by the Divine nature within us and we repent, however, the non-Christian refuses to repent, therefore we can say that the root of sin is not destroyed in this person, they 'continue in sin', in rebellion to God. In this sense, the Christian cannot continue to sin, he cannot live in rebellion to his Lord for that rebellion has been destroyed.

This fact is also another of John's marks of a true Christian and the reason I believe it is not possible to know Christ as Savior whilst rejecting Him as Lord. There must be a death to self, a death to the ego! This third interpretation encompasses what John is saying and raises questions about those who claim to be Christians, yet can continue to live in sinful rebellion.

Therefore, let's examine the following question. Is there a biblical difference between a 'believer' and a 'disciple'?

This letter of John's is a case in point, for the apostle recognizes that there are many who claim to be Christians but are not, such is the reason John has given us so many marks of a true Christian; He intends for us to examine ourselves.

Those who teach that one can be a believer, apart from being a disciple, have, frankly speaking, no idea of what Scripture refers to as a believer. The very word 'faith', from which 'believer' comes, has within its meaning to 'cast our whole weight upon'. Faith is never just an intellectual assent to something or someone, it must be a surrender to the will of God or it is merely the desire to have salvation whilst continuing to rule our own lives.

This topic is discussed fully in the first chapter of my small book *Running the Race* which is available free from my website, www.stevecopland.com, so here I will give just a few illustrations.

Jesus gave many examples within His parables, and the lives of those He met, in reference to what salvation requires. Take for example the parable of the sower and the seed from Matthew 13. In this parable Jesus gives us an explanation of His teaching. The seed fell upon four kinds of paths, rocky places and soil, but only one group of seeds put down deep roots to salvation and discipleship.

In the first three examples, the person, representing those who heard the message of the gospel, either did not fully understand the message or did not consider the cost of discipleship. None of them bore any fruit. Only the fourth group *'heard the word and understood'* (13:23) and these ones produced a crop. Can a person be called a 'believer', a Christian, and bear no fruit? The answer is 'no', for 'by their fruit you will recognize' true Christians, and those who do not bear fruit will be 'cut down and thrown into the fire' (Matthew 7:18-20). The parable of the vine has a similar meaning.

Likewise, in Luke 14:25-35, Jesus outlines the cost of becoming a disciple. Great crowds were following Him to receive what they could from Him. Many had received healing or had been fed in the miracles Jesus performed when there was no food. We could say that they 'believed' in what He could do, but were they true followers, were they disciples? It was to these that He spoke of discipleship, of the cost of following Him.

The NT speaks of 'belonging to Christ' (Romans 8:9), of 'being God's own possession' (Ephesians 1:14), the proof of which is in whether or not we have been born again by receiving the Holy Spirit within us. If He is not present we will not produce the 'fruits of the Spirit', for He is the source of these fruits, and therefore, without such fruit we do not belong to Him but are still ruling our own lives.

This teaching is consistent throughout the NT. In Romans 10:5-13 Paul outlines the necessity of confessing Christ as Lord in order to be saved. He speaks of both the heart and mouth. Believing in the heart is not enough, we must also confess that Christ is our Lord. In Colossians 2:6-7 Paul makes it absolutely clear that receiving Christ as Lord is fundamental to both our initial experience of salvation, and ongoing experience of sanctification, growing in discipleship. He says:

So then, just as you received Christ Jesus as Lord, continue to live in him, 7 rooted and strengthened in the faith as you were taught, and overflowing with thankfulness.

The early Church made no distinction between believer and disciple as they are one and the same. Counting the cost of salvation before surrendering our wills to God is not a works-based theology, indeed, surrender is completely the opposite of works for it is a letting go of control into the Lordship of Christ. Such a person no longer has the root of sin within them, a rebellion to rule their own life, and although they may slip and fall on occasions, they will be quick to confess their sins and submit once again to the Lord. This is John's message in a nutshell.

Summary

The passage we have been studying claims that those who are born of God, born again, cannot continue in sin. John is never saying that born again Christians never commit sins, but rather that they can never continue to live in rebellion against the will of God. The keys to understanding this passage correctly are in the words 'rebellion', (lawlessness) and 'continue'.

Rebellion against God is rooted in the human ego, the self-ruling principle, and it is the ego which has been crucified with Christ in a disciple of Christ. The self-centered ego dies when a person submits their will to the will of God, and in this sense a person is no longer a slave to sin, indeed, Paul says we should consider such people 'dead to sin' (Romans 6). Yet the sinful nature remains and Christians sometimes fall to its desires. The proof that one is truly born again, the evidence that Christ is Lord, is twofold.

1. The Divine nature within convicts the person that they must repent, confess their sins, and be 'cleansed from all unrighteousness' (1John 1:8-9). Unless the Christian does this, the Holy Spirit will continue to convict and the Christian will have no peace or joy until confession and forgiveness have occurred. In this sense, they cannot 'continue' in sin, for their ego has already been crucified, it is dead, and the indwelling Spirit of God commands them to obey. A disobedient Christian is the most miserable of people.

2. The person who claims to be a Christian but can happily live with unconfessed sin, proves that the Holy Spirit does not dwell within them. Without the indwelling Divine nature the ego is still alive and controlling this person. In this sense they continue in sin, in rebellion, in lawlessness, they are still their own master, Christ is not Lord. In essence, they are not born again and their sin will lead to eternal death (1 John 5:16-18). If He is not Lord, He is not living within where He has absolute right to convict them. They do not hear His voice because they are not His sheep.

John calls us to examine ourselves in order to determine whether or not the root of sin is still alive or has been crucified with Christ, whether or not we are simply intellectual 'believers', or true disciples who daily deny our sinful natures and carry our cross with the joy and peace that only Christ can give.

Study Thirteen

The Tenth Mark: Love in Action

1st John 3:16-20 and 4:7-19

In this study we will examine two similar passages where John explains the link between God's love and those who are born again.

3:14 We know that we have passed from death to life, because we love our brothers. Anyone who does not love remains in death. 15 Anyone who hates his brother is a murderer, and you know that no murderer has eternal life in him. 16 This is how we know what love is: Jesus Christ laid down his life for us. And we ought to lay down our lives for our brothers.

17 If anyone has material possessions and sees his brother in need but has no pity on him, how can the love of God be in him? 18 Dear children, let us not love with words or tongue but with actions and in truth. 19 This then is how we know that we belong to the truth, and how we set our hearts at rest in his presence 20 whenever our hearts condemn us. For God is greater than our hearts, and he knows everything.

4:7 Dear friends, let us love one another, for love comes from God. Everyone who loves has been born of God and knows God. 8 Whoever does not love does not know God, because God is love. 9 This is how God showed his love among us: He sent his one and only Son into the world that we might live through him. 10 This is love: not that we loved God, but that he loved us and sent his Son as an atoning sacrifice for our sins.

11 Dear friends, since God so loved us, we also ought to love one another. 12 No one has ever seen God; but if we love each other, God lives in us and his love is made complete in us. 13 We know that we live in him and he is us, because he has given us of his Spirit. 14 And we have seen and testify that the Father has sent his Son to be the Savior of the world.

15 If anyone acknowledges that Jesus is the Son of God, God lives in him and he in God. 16 And so we know and rely on the love God has for us.

In the New Testament there are four Greek words translated as 'love', all of which have quite different meanings and emphases. They are as follows:

1. Agape: Agape is Divine love, a love which is both unconditional and has self-sacrifice as its foundation. Agape love is never conditioned upon the merit of the recipient. God is Love (agape). This form of sacrificial love is always active.

2. Phileo: Phileo is the love of companionship, or 'brotherly love'. Being built upon relationships, it is not unconditional and may end if the relationship ends.

3. Storge: Storge may be defined as a natural affection or obligation, such as in relationships between parents and children, husbands and wives.

4: Eros. Eros is romantic or erotic love, a form of passion which is often selfish, a shallow form of love driven by hormones, emotions, and/or a need to feel loved and accepted.

Those without Christ can and do experience phileo, storge and eros forms of love, but without the indwelling Divine nature we cannot experience agape love, for this form of love has its source in the Divine nature. In the two passages we are studying, John is speaking of agape love, and he points us directly to the action of God's love in sending His Son into the world as a sacrifice for sin.

How often do we really stop and contemplate the depth of verses like John 3:16, and those above, which speak of God giving His only Son? As human beings we often enjoy comparing ourselves to others, usually with those we deem less than ourselves, but what if we compare ourselves to the heart of God?

If you were the ruler of a great nation, as God is Creator of this world, how would you act? Imagine your subjects rejected your laws and committed atrocities in your name, imagine they chose the most evil of your enemies and invited them into the land and served them, even sacrificed their children to them. Imagine that these people raped and murdered, starved and oppressed the weak, perverted the innocent and even denied your very existence.

And imagine you had ten legions of mighty warriors, like the angels of God, who could annihilate all of your enemies in a single day and restore order. And that you also had but one child, a godly, obedient Son who was willing to do whatever you asked of Him.

If it were up to us, I imagine we would destroy every enemy, bringing swift justice down upon their heads and show mercy only to those who had at least resisted the evil offered to them, or the few who tried to remain pure. But *God so loved the world* and all of the people of this world, that He gave His precious Son in order that He might save all of them, even the most vile of His enemies. He put the punishment that we so rightly deserved onto Jesus, He watched His Son die a horrific death so that we could be forgiven, even though at the time we were not even seeking His mercy and forgiveness. That is agape love in action!

Agape love is more than an attribute of God, it is the core of God, it is who He is. God is not merely loving, rather, He *is* love, its very source, along with His being the source of perfect holiness, justice, mercy, etc. All of these exist because He exists; they are that which describe who the Triune God is, and they are demonstrated in His holy, loving, merciful justice through the sacrifice of Jesus Christ on the cross of Calvary.

Therefore, John argues, if this same Divine nature lives permanently within us, the proof of that will be in how we act toward others. Notice John's emphasis in the first passage:

3:14 We know that we have passed from death to life, because we love our brothers. Anyone who does not love remains in death. 15 Anyone who hates his brother is a murderer, and you know that no murderer has eternal life in him. 16 This is how we know what love is: Jesus Christ laid down his life for us. And we ought to lay down our lives for our brothers.

17 If anyone has material possessions and sees his brother in need but has no pity on him, how can the love of God be in him? 18 Dear children, let us not love with words or tongue but with actions and in truth. 19 This then is how we know that we belong to the truth, and how we set our hearts at rest in his presence 20 whenever our hearts condemn us. For God is greater than our hearts, and he knows everything.

The proof that we have passed from death to life, (are partakers of the Divine nature) is demonstrated in our love for one another. Indeed, if we do not have this love, we 'remain in death', we are not born again. John tells us that if we hate our brother we are a murderer. The word hate (*miseo*) can be used to speak of emotions, but is more commonly used as an opposite to agape love. Love acts, but hate refuses to act.

Jesus used this example when speaking of counting the cost of discipleship in Luke 14 when He spoke of hating mother, father, children and even one's own life. His point was not that we should have feelings of hatred towards those closest to us in order to become a disciple, but rather, in order to take up our cross we must be willing to turn our backs on all we hold dear or we will not be ready to die to self.

John's point is similar. Agape love compels us to loving actions. Hating our brother, in this context, simply means that we turn our back on him, we refuse to act in love, we don't care if he lives or dies. John goes on to use the example of Christ who lay down His life for us, and calls us to do the same. Does he mean that we must be willing to die for our brothers and sisters in Christ? Perhaps he does have this in mind, although this would be an extreme circumstance, but from the next verses John reveals his intentions.

17 If anyone has material possessions and sees his brother in need but has no pity on him, how can the love of God be in him? 18 Dear children, let us not love with words or tongue but with actions and in truth.

There is no ambiguity here. If we can see a brother or sister in need and ignore that need whilst we have the means to help them, then by what criteria do we claim to be Christian? Agape love compels us to act, therefore, a lack of action demonstrates the absence of agape love. John goes on to claim that this is how we know that we *belong to the truth*, and moreover, that loving actions set our hearts at peace in the Lord's presence because the Lord knows our hearts. Therefore, our action or inaction, in this context, can either condemn or bring us peace.

The second passage is a form of summary.

4:7 Dear friends, let us love one another, for love comes from God. Everyone who loves has been born of God and knows God. 8 Whoever does not love does not know God, because God is love. 9 This is how God showed his love among us: He sent his one and only Son into the world that we might live through him. 10 This is love: not that we loved God, but that he loved us and sent his Son as an atoning sacrifice for our sins.

11 Dear friends, since God so loved us, we also ought to love one another. 12 No one has ever seen God; but if we love each other, God lives in us and his love is made complete in us. 13 We know that we live in him and he is us, because he has given us of his Spirit. 14 And we have seen and testify that the Father has sent his Son to be the Savior of the world.

15 If anyone acknowledges that Jesus is the Son of God, God lives in him and he in God. 16 And so we know and rely on the love God has for us.

John categorically states that *everyone who loves* (with agape love) *has been born of God and knows God.* If agape love is absent in a person's life, this will be most obvious through their actions, or more specifically, inaction, for as Christians our lives must imitate the life of Christ who acted in sacrificial love for us.

Summary

The practical reality of John's challenge is an everyday occurrence in the country where I serve the Lord, Ukraine. There are many poor and needy people here, including Christians, but for the most part, the Body of Christ acts in agape love. The 'prosperity gospel', which I consider absolutely unbiblical, is almost non-existent in Ukraine and other countries which have similar levels of poverty. On the contrary, the mistaken teaching that the Lord desires His children to be wealthy beyond their needs is actually a way of justifying greed.

The Body of Christ is spread throughout the world, indeed, our brothers and sisters in Christ are not simply those sitting besides us in church, but all who have surrendered their lives to Christ. When I witness the levels of greed and selfishness which is prevalent in so many Western mega-churches who teach 'prosperity', I find myself asking if they are Christian in any real sense of the word.

The book of Acts records how Paul collected money for the poor who were suffering the effects of drought,

Christians from different countries making sacrifices for their fellow Christians. Yet we witness so-called Christian leaders in Western countries hoarding millions, living in mansions, flying in private jets and boasting of their wealth whilst Christians in poor countries suffer extreme conditions. Some even have the audacity (or level of biblical hatred) to preach their erroneous doctrines in poverty stricken countries, collect offerings from the poor, and return to their mansions richer than they were before.

John asks the question, *how can the love of God be in them*, and the obvious answer is that, either they are terribly deceived, or they do not know Christ at all. We are to be in this world but not of this world, we are called to love as God loves, we are commanded to love one another as brothers and sisters in Christ.

If our 'love' is merely in words rather than action and truth, then we have no foundation upon which we may claim to be in Christ, no demonstrative proof that the Divine nature dwells within us, for agape love is always love in action.

Study Fourteen

The Eleventh Mark: God-fearing, yet Perfect in
Love.

1st John 4:16-19

*4:16 And so we rely on the love God has for us. God
is love. Whoever lives in love lives in God, and God in
him. 17 Love is made complete among us so that we will
have confidence on the day of judgment, because in this
world we are like him. 18 There is no fear in love. But
perfect love drives out fear, because fear has to do with
punishment. The man who fears is not made perfect in
love. 19 We love because he first loved us.*

The Scriptures have a great deal to say on the topic
of fearing God, especially in the Old Testament, yet
there is also a lot of confusion within the Church as to
how Christians should understand this topic.

In the text of this study, John tells us that there is *no
fear in love,* that *perfect love drives out fear, because
fear has to do with punishment.* Many understand this to
mean that Christians should have absolutely no fear of
God, yet in the Book of Acts, after the deaths of Ananias
and Sapphira, we read that *great fear seized the whole
church and all who heard about these events (Acts 5:11)*
and several years later, after the conversion of Saul we
read;

*Then the church throughout Judea, Galilee and
Samaria enjoyed a time of peace. It was strengthened:*

134

and encouraged by the Holy Spirit, it grew in numbers, living in the fear of the Lord (Acts 9:31).

The apostle Paul told the Philippians; *continue to work out your salvation with fear and trembling (Phil 2:12)* and Peter wrote that we should *show proper respect to everyone: Love the brotherhood of believers, fear God, honor the king(1st Peter 2:17).*

On the surface of it, there may seem to be something of a contradiction here. Consider also the testimony of John in Revelation. The same John who called himself the *disciple that Jesus loved (John 13:23, 21:20)* and who wrote that *there is no fear in love,* tells us in Revelation 1:12-17 that, when he saw the vision of Jesus while on the island of Patmos, he *fell at his feet as though dead.* The Lord placed His right hand on John and told him *do not be afraid.*

John lived with Jesus for three years. He witnessed the humanity of Jesus and the awesome power of God in the miracles Jesus performed. He was there on the mountain when Jesus was transfigured, he reclined against Jesus at the Last Supper, He watched Him die on the cross and saw the risen Christ, even ate with Jesus after He resurrected. John was on the island of Patmos because of his testimony of Christ, and we can be confident in saying that John had no fear of the wrath of God, that he understood that *perfect love drives out fear,* yet when he saw Jesus in His post-ascension glory, he fell down as if dead, he fainted at the sight, and the Lord told him not to be afraid (Rev 1:17).

Why was John afraid? The answer to that question is in reading John's description (Revelation 1:12ff) of what the Lord looked like. John heard a voice, he turned

135

around and saw someone 'like a son of man' standing among seven golden lampstands, dressed in a robe reaching to his feet, a golden sash around His chest, with head and hair as white as snow, eyes like blazing fire, feet glowing like bronze in a furnace, a voice like the sound of rushing water, holding seven stars in His right hand, a sharp double edged sword proceeding from His mouth, and a face shining like the brilliance of the sun. I think it is fair to say that this image was not the same as how he remembered Jesus on the day he watched Him ascend into heaven.

As we continue to read John's account, the Lord explains the meaning of the stars and sword, and gives John messages to the seven churches. After this (chapter 4) John sees a door opened and he is taken up to the throne room of God where he witnessed flashes of lighting, rumblings and peels of thunder, a testimony similar to that of the Israelites who stood at the foot of Mount Sinai in Exodus 19 and 20, the day God gave them the Ten Commandments through the mouth of Moses.

On that day, Moses told them: *Do not be afraid. God has come to test you, so that the fear of the Lord will be with you to keep you from sinning (Exodus 20:20).* John witnesses four living creatures and twenty-four elders around the throne of God, worshipping as their voices cried out; *Holy, holy, holy is the Lord God Almighty, who was, and is, and is to come.*

All of these observations point towards the same conclusions; the holiness of God, and the sinfulness of humanity. At Mount Sinai God was demonstrating the difference between Himself and every false god, namely that He alone is holy. The ancients offered sacrifices to idols, not because they saw themselves as sinners, but rather to appease the gods who might withhold the rains, destroy crops, and diminish their fertility. In the minds of these idol worshippers the concept of sin was fundamentally absent.

Their gods were not interested in holiness, but were understood to be capricious beings who demanded worship to caress their egos. Many were dead stone or wood, but others were of demonic origin (Deuteronomy 32:17), fallen creatures who endowed false prophets with power in exchange for human sacrifice and acts of debauchery.

At Mount Sinai the One True God was revealing Himself to fallen humanity, revealing that He is Holy, He is the essence and source of holiness. The fear of the Lord is the fear of absolute holiness, it is the knowledge that God can never compromise with sin, and the revelation that we are fallen creatures, that *all have sinned and fall short of the glory of God (Romans 3:23).*

And this is why *the fear of the Lord is the beginning of wisdom, and knowledge of the Holy One is understanding (Proverbs 9:10).* It is not until we begin to understand God's holiness, and our sinfulness, that we can begin to understand mercy, justice, atonement, and that *without the shedding of blood there is no forgiveness of sins (Hebrews 9:22).*

Therefore, we can conclude that without understanding the fear of the Lord we cannot understand the cross of Christ, for it is in the cross that the holiness of God and atonement for sin are reconciled.

With this understanding, and recognizing that the Old Testament verses point to Jesus Christ, we can read such verses in a new light. Consider the following examples:

The fear of the Lord leads to life (Proverbs 19:23).

It is in recognizing the holiness of God and His wrath towards sin that we come to the conviction and understanding that we are sinners in need of a Savior. In this way the fear of the Lord leads to life, eternal life for those who trust in Christ for salvation.

The Lord delights in those who fear him, who put their hope in his unfailing love (Psalm 147:11).

The Father has poured out His wrath towards sin onto His beloved Son. In this act He has demonstrated His hatred for sin and love for lost sinners. For God *so loved the world* of lost sinners, that He gave His only Son. He delights in those who have put their hope in Christ, in His unfailing love.

The Lord confides in those who fear him; he makes his covenant known to them (Psalm 25:14).

In the Old Testament God made His covenant known to those who fear Him, demonstrating the outworking of that first covenant of the law in the sacrifices offered in the temple, the sins placed upon the scapegoat, and witnessed at the mercy seat where reconciliation is revealed. All of this pointed to the new covenant, made possible by the blood of Jesus Christ and inaugurated on the Day of Pentecost, an eternal covenant made known through the witness of the indwelling Holy Spirit (Romans 8:16).

There is no contradiction regarding the fear of the Lord in the New Testament. John's statements in the text we are studying have a very specific context, namely, that those who *rely on the love God has for us*, a love demonstrated in the cross, need never fear God's wrath, for we have passed from wrath into life. It is Christ alone who has declared us to be perfect in Him (Hebrews 10:14), hidden in Him (Colossians 3:3), and in Him we are *made perfect in love*, because *he first loved us*.

We continue in that love, unafraid of God's wrath and trusting in Christ, yet we live each day knowing that we live in His grace. We have *been made perfect* (justified), solely by the blood of Christ, and are *being made perfect* (sanctified) as we live in obedience, this is the meaning of this verse in Hebrews 10:14.

Is God still Angry?

In the last decade or so, especially amongst those leading the 'Emergent Church' movement, such as Rob Bell, is this idea that God no longer has wrath towards sin, that God is no longer angry, and therefore, there is no need for anyone to fear His wrath. This view is absolutely false, unbiblical, and extremely dangerous on every level and for the following reasons.

1. It is absolutely false because it denies the fundamental fact that God is the same yesterday, today and forever. It is false because it splits the Bible, not in regards to covenants, but in regards to the character of God. It recognizes the wrath of God within Old

Testament history, but claims that in Jesus Christ God's wrath has been replaced with love. In this sense it not only divides the Triune nature of God in the extreme, but suggests that God has changed, He has matured from wrath to love. Such a theology must think Paul, Peter, James, and the writer of Hebrews, were fools to remind us of the wrath of God towards sin, or that our God *is a consuming fire* (Hebrews 12:29).

2. It is unbiblical for the reasons above, but more so, it fundamentally rejects any notion of Divine punishment, of hell, and strongly suggests that God can compromise with sin because of the cross. The absolute opposite is true! Throughout the book of Hebrews the writer's intentions are clear. He explains the reasons for animal sacrifices, yet shows that God's wrath was not satisfied, therefore, God poured out His wrath upon His beloved Son at a cost no human being can begin to comprehend.

But what, the author asks, will happen to those who reject what the Lord has given in the cross? Yes, God's wrath against sin was great, but His wrath against those who reject His offer of forgiveness in Christ will be overwhelmingly greater (Hebrews 10).

Scripture tells us that the most frightening demonstration of God's wrath is still in the future, that which we refer to as The Great Tribulation. The Great Flood destroyed every breathing creature within 40 days, but the Great Tribulation will take up to seven years. Those seven years will witness devastation and wrath on a scale never before seen in the history of the world, and never to be repeated. And when Jesus Christ returns we will witness the resurrection of all people (Acts 24:15), the Judgment, and the reality of hell.

3. It is dangerous because it paints a totally false picture in regards to the unchanging character of God and opens the door to pluralism, suggesting that, because God is no longer angry towards sin, that any person of any religion may rest assured that there will be no punishment for rejecting Christ. Indeed, this is fundamentally what the emergent church movement promotes, despite Jesus many warnings to the contrary.

Most of those who teach such false doctrine claim that, even after the return of Christ, there will be opportunity for unbelievers to change their minds, in fact, God will keep the door of the New Jerusalem open for all eternity. If we are to accept this teaching, we are forced to believe that Jesus was completely mistaken about hell, that there is no one suffering in Hades presently, and no person will be thrown into Gehenna after judgment. For all of the above reasons, I reject these teachings completely, as must every Christian who takes God's Word seriously.

Summary

God is the same today, yesterday, and forever. His wrath towards sin is uncompromising, His wrath towards those who reject His mercy offered in the sacrifice of His Son, frightening beyond imagination, as those who experience the Great Tribulation will discover. Should Christians fear God? If we are speaking of fearing God's wrath, the answer is no, but if stating that we recognize the unchanging, uncompromising holiness of God and His wrath towards the sin of rejecting Christ, the answer is yes.

John says that *we rely on the love God has for us*, because we rely absolutely on the cross of Christ, and in Christ we are made perfect in His love. For this reason we have no fear of punishment, for we stand in reverent humility before our crucified Savior, acknowledging our sin, His merciful love, and unfailing faithfulness.

We who are in Christ have passed from wrath into life eternal, and in this we rejoice, yet in our hearts must be ever present gratitude for the Lord's mercy, and a holy reverence for what it cost our Lord and Savior to bring us into His eternal family.

These verses of John's challenge us to reflect on our salvation. If we still fear God's wrath then we should ask ourselves if we have truly experienced new birth, for new birth drives out fear and makes us confident, not in ourselves, but in what has been done for us. To continue to fear God's wrath after receiving salvation is to insult the cross of Christ and refuse to believe the Lord's promise. Such a person cannot experience perfect love in this state, for unbelief has overtaken faith.

If you find yourself in this position, repent of your unbelief and meditate on the cross, on Christ crucified, and when His Spirit has opened your eyes to Christ's finished work, surrender to Him absolutely. Salvation is wholly the work of Jesus Christ, it begins and ends in Him. Our part, like the thief who hung next to our Lord, is to place our lives in His hands, even if that life is about to expire. The thief had nothing to offer but faith in who Christ is, he believed, and that very day was taken with his Lord into paradise. He died relying on the love of Christ, and we must live every day in the same way.

Study Fifteen

Answered Prayer

1st John 5:14-15

14 This is the assurance we have in approaching God: that if we ask anything according to his will, he hears us. 15 And if we know that he hears us - whatever we ask - we know that we have what we asked of him.

For many, the topic of prayer remains one of the great mysteries of the Christian life. Christians of different denominations have extremely diverse opinions about how prayer and faith work together. Let me give two extreme examples.

Those who lean towards hyper-Calvinism push the sovereignty of God to such an extreme that I wonder why they pray at all. If life is completely predetermined and no creature can ever go against the will of God, then logically, prayer cannot change anything. For such people, prayer is just agreeing with whatever is happening, because whatever is happening must be God's will, because nothing happens outside of His will.

In the other extreme are the Charismatic 'name it and claim it' people who believe that faith is claiming whatever you imagine God wants you to have. If you don't get what you asked for, it isn't because your desire is outside of God's will, but because you allowed doubt to make your prayer powerless.

Christians from both of these extremes can find verses which they claim support their particular theology. The Calvinist will quote something like Romans 9:19ff where Paul argues with those who ask *'who resists his will'*. They will point out that Psalm 115:3 tells us that *'our God is in the heavens; he does what he pleases'*.

The Charismatic may quote John 15:7, that *'if you remain in me and my words remain in you, ask whatever you wish, and it will be given you'*, or John 14:14 where Jesus says *'you may ask me for anything in my name, and I will do it'*.

I reject both of these extremes, not only because they are immature and unbiblical, but more importantly, they fundamentally destroy the entire purpose of prayer! In both of these extremes the Christian's relationship with God appears almost non-existent. Why? What kind of a relationship does a person have with the Lord if they believe that every detail of life is predetermined? Is this a Father/child relationship, or a Master/puppet relationship? And what kind of a relationship does a person have with the Lord if they believe that they can make Him do whatever they wish? Both of these views are a horrid distortion of the relationship the Lord desires us to have with Him.

To the hyper-Calvinist I would ask this. Is God allowed to change His mind, change His plans when asked by a person who knows and loves Him? In Numbers 14 the Israelites rebelled against the Lord. He told Moses that He would *'strike them down with a plague and destroy them'* (v12). But Moses replied that the nations who had witnessed God leading Israel would say *'the Lord was not able to bring these people into the land he promised them on oath; so he slaughtered them in the desert'* (v16). Moses asked Him to forgive the people. The Lord changed His mind. He forgave the people, but none of those who rebelled entered the Promised Land.

And to the Charismatics I would ask this. Is the Lord not allowed to refuse your requests? Is He not the Lord of *your* life, the one to whom you surrendered *your* will? James would tell you that *'you do not receive because you ask with wrong motives...'* (James 4:3). The Lord is not some genie in a bottle who must grant our requests if we ask in a particular way or 'name it and claim it'!

If you claim that Jesus Christ is the Lord of your life, and that you desire to walk as Jesus walked, becoming increasingly Christ-like, then understand that Jesus was perfected through His sufferings (Hebrews 2: 10, 18) and Paul tells us that if we are God's children then *we are heirs - heirs of God and co-heirs with Christ, if indeed we share in his sufferings in order that we may also share in his glory (Romans 8:17).* If your relationship with God is based on Him making your life easy and prosperous, then you should ask yourself if your God is the God of Scripture or one you have created in your imagination.

In this letter of John's there is little about prayer. In the first chapter he tells us to confess our sins, and in the last chapter we have the two verses of this study and the verses we will examine in our next study. However, in his gospel John records many of Jesus instructions and promises regarding prayer, and an entire chapter of Jesus praying to the Father (Chapter 17). For me, the two verses we are studying in this letter are a statement of John's understanding of every word Jesus said about prayer, therefore, let's look at some of the verses in his gospel and compare them with the statement in this letter.

13 And I will do whatever you ask in my name, so that the Son may bring glory to the Father. 14 You may ask for anything in my name, and I will do it (John 14:13-14).

These two verses are in the context of Jesus comforting His disciples after telling them that He will soon be leaving them. Philip asked that Jesus show them the Father, and Jesus explains that *anyone who has seen me has seen the Father.* He goes on to tell them that the words He speaks are not just His own, but rather *it is the Father living in me, who is doing his work.* Jesus is about to tell the disciples that they will be filled with the Divine nature, Father, Son and Holy Spirit.

When this occurs they may make requests of Him and He will do as they ask. Why does He give them this assurance? Because when they are filled with the Divine nature they will be as He is at that moment, the Godhead will be living in them and doing His work. Like Him, their words will not just be their own, but His words.

They will ask *in his name* so that they may also bring glory to the Father. The term *'in his name'* means 'in his authority', or 'on his behalf'. In ancient times a king would send an emissary or ambassador and this chosen person had the authority to speak in the king's name. The emissary spoke the king's will on his behalf. This is the authority Jesus is promising here. When the Divine nature dwells within us we have the authority to speak on the Lord's behalf, not words or ideas of our own, but conveying *His* will.

146

7 If you remain in me and my words remain in you, ask whatever you wish, and it will be given you. 8 This is to my Father's glory, that you may bear much fruit, showing yourselves to be my disciples (John 15:7-8).

These verses are almost a summary of what we have just said. Notice it is Jesus' words which remain in us, and with His words we may ask whatever we wish. Again, these verses explain that we are asking as He wills us to ask and, as in the previous passage, it is for the Father's glory. Christ's words and will within us producing fruit for the Father's glory.

16 You did not choose me, but I chose you to go and bear fruit - fruit that will last. Then the Father will give you whatever you ask in my name.

Notice again the pre-eminence of Christ in this passage. It is He who chose, it is His will that we are chosen to bear fruit. The fruit is the fruit of the Spirit, and those who are producing this fruit do so because the Spirit leads them. Such people will receive whatever they ask because they ask through the Spirit.

24 Until now you have not asked for anything in my name. Ask and you will receive, and your joy will be complete (John 16:24).

In the beginning of chapter sixteen Jesus is speaking of the work of the Holy Spirit. He tells them that the Spirit will *guide them into all truth,* will *not speak on his own,* but *take from what is mine and make it known to you.* As in the previous passages, the context is the same. Being filled with the Holy Spirit they will know God's will and ask accordingly.

None of the passages above ever hint at the possibility that we will receive anything other than that which the Spirit puts in our hearts to pray for. All of the verses in John's gospel are saying exactly the same as in his letter, the former are Jesus' words, and the latter John's understanding. Let's return to the verses of this study.

14 This is the assurance we have in approaching God: that if we ask anything according to his will, he hears us. 15 And if we know that he hears us - whatever we ask - we know that we have what we asked of him.

For me, these two verses summarize exactly what John understands as our relationship with the Lord in prayer. Throughout his letter John has given us eleven marks of a true disciple of Christ, and He will give one more. If we have read this far and know that we are truly in Christ, and Christ in us, then we have the anointing of the Spirit, we have no fear of punishment in approaching God's throne in prayer, and we come knowing that He hears us when we are in His will, and that we are assured of receiving our request in accord with His will.

The fundamental point is simply this! Those who are truly in Christ always desire the will of God in their lives. This is the foundation of our faith, that we trust the Lord's will for our lives, even when at times we cannot understand, or when His will is difficult. We approach Him as those who have been *made perfect in love* and we trust in His love for us *because he first loved us (4:18-19).*

Summary

When we are speaking of knowing the will of God it can, for many of us, be something of a mystery. Within the pages of Scripture we witness, especially through the works of the prophets and words of Jesus, that the Lord has a sovereign plan for this world He created. That plan will be completed exactly as foretold. God's sovereign plan is foretold outside of our understanding of time, it is a revealing of His foreknowledge and something mere humans cannot fully comprehend.

However, we also know without doubt that He walks with us within time, revealing His will for us as individual children. Can our prayers persuade Him? The answer must be yes, for apart from His overarching sovereign will there is His personal permissible will, as the story of Moses reveals.

Added to this is the fact that the Lord works with us in partnership. Human beings have an important part to play in both God's sovereign plan, and His plan for us as individuals. We are told throughout the New Testament that we make choices in how we live for Christ, we are encouraged to be faithful and obedient, for our actions have consequences. We are also told in Ephesians 2:10 that *we are God's workmanship, created in Christ Jesus to do good works, which God prepared in advance for us to do.*

In order to fulfill those 'good works' we may have to be tested through suffering and trials, and sometimes

149

those trials seem too much to bear. But we should never lose faith and hope during these times, for the Lord will never place before us something we cannot achieve in Him. This is the practical outworking of our relationship, His leading, our trusting. Paul referred to this as 'strict training' when writing of his life as an apostle and the reward waiting for him. He used the following analogy;

Everyone who competes in the games goes into strict training. They do it to get a crown that will not last; but we do it to get a crown that will last forever (1 Corinthians 9:25).

We began out walk with Christ by coming to the cross with open hands, surrendering all that we are and have to His will. We surrendered to Him knowing that He loves us beyond anything we can imagine. Come to Him every day with open hands. Ask Him to place in your hands whatever is in His will and plan for your life, and to take out anything which is not His will, anything which may hinder that plan. This, in essence, is 'walking in the Spirit'.

There will be many times when walking in the Lord's will is humanly difficult, but know that such times are planned for us in order that our joy may be complete. And remember that *blessed is the man who perseveres under trial, for when he has stood the test, he will receive the crown of life that God has promised to all who love him (James1:12).*

Study Sixteen

Sin that leads to death

1st John 5: 16-19

16 If anyone sees his brother commit a sin that does not lead to death, he should pray and God will give him life. I refer to those whose sin does not lead to death. There is a sin that leads to death. I am not saying he should pray about that. 17 All wrongdoing is sin, and there is sin that does not lead to death. 18 We know that anyone born of God does not continue to sin; the one who was born of God keeps him safe, and the evil one does not touch him. 19 We know that we are children of God, and that the whole world is under the control of the evil one.

The verses above are considered to be some of the most difficult to understand in the New Testament, perhaps because many Christians believe that all sin has equal and eternal consequences. The fundamental questions we will ask in the study are as follows. Is John referring to physical or spiritual death, or does he allude to both in these verses? Why would John suggest that there is a form of sin that we shouldn't pray about?

Physical Death

Throughout the commandments of the Law of God found in Leviticus and Deuteronomy, the Lord gave Moses instructions regarding punishments for various acts of sin. Punishments for certain sins, such as knocking out a person's tooth or eye, required compensation and forms of penance. Certain sexual sins, such as sexual relations with one's aunt or uncle would leave the couple barren and childless (Lev 20:19-20) and often excommunicated from the community of Israel. In the case of gross sins such as adultery, incest, sex with animals, child sacrifice or marrying a woman and her daughter, the penalty was death by stoning or burning.

The legal systems of most countries also differentiate between serious and minor crimes and try to ensure that 'the punishment fits the crime', albeit capital punishment has been abandoned in most Western countries. Therefore, from a purely physical perspective there are sins which lead to death and sins which carry lesser punishments.

From a New Testament perspective we have several examples of Christians sinning in such a way that their sin led to physical death. In Acts 5 there is the account of Ananias and Sapphira who 'lied to the Holy Spirit' (v3) and both died as a result of this act of deceit. Also, in 1st Corinthians 11 Paul is rebuking Christians for their licentious behavior during the Lord's Supper. These Christians had turned grace into a license for sin, an early branch of Gnosticism, and were using the wine and bread which symbolized Christ's death and new covenant, in an 'unworthy manner', in gluttony and drunkenness.

Paul tells them they are *'guilty of sinning against the body and blood of the Lord' (v27)* and explains to them, *'that is why many among you are weak and sick, and a number of you have fallen asleep'.* Paul is explaining why some of them had died prematurely, and many of them were on their way to physical death if they did not examine themselves and repent.

Although we have these examples in the New Testament I am certain that John is not referring to physical death in the verses of our study for several reasons, but mainly because of his words, *there is a sin that leads to death. I am not saying he should pray about that*. John's words here could be paraphrased as 'I am not saying you can pray with any assurance of God's promise". Remember John's instructions on prayer from the previous study on the verses which precede these. John says;

14 This is the assurance we have in approaching God: that if we ask anything according to his will, he hears us. 15 And if we know that he hears us - whatever we ask - we know that we have what we asked of him.(1 John 5:14-15)

The only reason John would suggest we not pray about something is if we knew that we could have no confidence in receiving a positive answer, because we could not know God's will. This could only be the case if there was no possibility of the sinning Christian repenting, something which contradicts John's teaching in chapter 3. Was that the case with the two examples of Christian sin we have just studied? If Ananias and his wife had fallen to their knees in sincere repentance, rather than upholding the lie before the apostles, I doubt they would have died instantly, and Paul was appealing to the Corinthians to repent. Therefore, if a brother or sister knew of the sins of either group, they could confidently pray for these Christians to repent and have hope that those prayers would be answered.

Spiritual Death

If the key to understanding the passage we are studying is in John's words *I am not saying he should pray about that*, and I believe it is, then we need to find examples within the New Testament where a person has committed a sin which, not only leads to eternal spiritual death (separation from God), but one that they can never repent of. If there is such a category of sin then John's words make sense, for it would be pointless to continue praying for such a person. There are two examples of sin which fall into this category within the New Testament. We will examine both. The first is found in Matthew 12:31-32.

31 And so I tell you, every sin and blasphemy will be forgiven men, but the blasphemy against the Spirit will not be forgiven. 32 Anyone who speaks a word against the Son of Man will be forgiven, but anyone who speaks against the Holy Spirit will not be forgiven, either in this age or in the age to come.

The words 'and so I tell you' mean that these two verses are both a conclusion and warning. Jesus has just healed a demon-possessed man who was both blind and mute (12:22). The people who saw the miracle asked 'Could this be the Son of David', meaning 'Is this the promised Messiah?' But the Pharisees were outraged and accused Jesus of casting out the demons with the power of Beelzebub (Satan). Verse 23 tells us that 'Jesus knew their thoughts', meaning that what they were thinking was even more vile and full of hatred than the words they had just spoken. He then explains about two kingdoms, the kingdom of Satan and the kingdom of God.

If Satan drives out Satan, then Satan's kingdom is divided against himself and his kingdom cannot stand. But if He (Jesus) is driving out demons by the Spirit of God, then the kingdom of God has come upon them, and the people are correct in discerning that the 'Son of David', the Messiah, is in their presence. Jesus then uses an analogy about robbing Satan's Kingdom and carrying off his possessions and ends with saying 'he who is with me is for me, and he do does not gather with me scatters'.

The Messiah had come to destroy Satan's kingdom and fulfill the prophecy of Genesis 3:15 of the 'Seed' who would crush the serpent's head. Christ's mission was to break the curse of death through His own death and resurrection, but God's kingdom would be established through the work of the Holy Spirit, the same work He had just demonstrated in the miracle.

Those who responded to the conviction of the Holy Spirit, repented and believed on Christ, would be filled with the Spirit, and these ones would rob the 'strong man's house', (bringing others out of Satan's kingdom through salvation in Christ) and in this way they would be 'gathering' the children of God. All of this work would be achieved through the coming of the Holy Spirit, the inauguration of the New Covenant.

So why is blasphemy against the Holy Spirit an unforgivable sin, and speaking against the Son of Man forgivable? Jesus came to testify of the coming kingdom, but even His own disciples doubted and fled. They saw miracle upon miracle, proof upon proof. Their faith was by sight, and the sight of His being crucified was too much for them. Even after seeing Him risen from death they went back to Galilee and their old ways of life.

All of that was forgivable because they were still acting in the flesh, not responding to the calling and conviction of the Holy Spirit. But when the Spirit came at Pentecost, they received Him because He opened their eyes to the truth and clarified everything they had seen in the flesh.

But what if, after that incredible revelation, they had refused to receive the Holy Spirit? If a person's mind and heart are opened by the Spirit so that they know Christ is God, they know they must repent and be saved, and yet they turn from Him or speak against Him, what else can the Lord do?

I have witnessed such people in my own life. I am not speaking of someone who casually rejects the gospel, but rather someone who was seeking God for months, who was brought right to the very foot of the cross, who understood through Divine revelation that they must surrender their will and walk away from their sin, but chose the sin. I have never seen any of them come back to the cross and never felt any more conviction to pray for them. This very process is discussed in Hebrews chapter 6, the second of our examples.

4 It is impossible for those who have once been enlightened, who have tasted the heavenly gift, who have shared in the Holy Spirit, 5 who have tasted the

156

goodness of the word of God and the powers of the coming age, 6 if they should fall away, to be brought back to repentance, because to their loss they are crucifying the Son of God all over again and subjecting him to public disgrace (Hebrews 6:4-6).

Firstly, some context. The Old Covenant of the Law was such an integral part of Jewish life that many Jews found it almost impossible to leave it behind. The Pharisees emphasized that salvation was by works of obedience to the Law, the keeping of holy days, performance of sacrifices, etc. But salvation in Christ is solely by grace through faith, not by works, but a gift from God (Ephesians 2:8). For people who had rigorously tried to keep the Law this New Covenant teaching was difficult. The entire book of Hebrews addresses this issue, encouraging Jews to leave the old behind and embrace the new.

But some, even after understanding, tasting and witnessing the promises of God in Christ, walked away and held onto the Old Covenant. The writer to the Hebrews says that it is 'impossible' to bring them back again to the foot of the cross. Some understand these verses in Hebrews to state clearly that these people were truly born again and lost their salvation. This is not the case, for several reasons.

Firstly, the text itself, and secondly, that this would contradict the rest of the New Testament. It is important to understand the choice of words of the author in order to grasp his intentions. If he wanted to state that these people were born of God, he would have used plain words such as 'for those who have believed, been saved, justified, born again, etc', but he purposely uses words which all mean to come on a journey of revelation all the way to the cross and then turn away without surrendering the will to God.

Let's examine the author's choice of words.

Once been enlightened. This refers to seeing the light, to having one's eyes opened to the truth, another way of speaking of the Holy Spirit's work of conviction and revelation (John 16:8) in preparation for salvation.

Tasted the heavenly gift. The author uses the word 'tasted' twice, both here and in verse 5 to speak of the word of God and powers of the coming age. Tasted is opposed to swallowed or accepted. It is like putting a strawberry on the lips, tasting it, before making a decision to eat it.

When a person is earnestly seeking God they experience this tasting as He leads them to the day of decision. The Lord does not command us to surrender our wills to Him without first teaching us to trust Him, opening our eyes to what He promises in the Scriptures (word), understanding what is to come, and tasting His presence. Like the children of Israel who experienced a multitude of miracles before coming to the Jordan, so the Lord leads us to that point of giving our lives to Him.

Shared in the Holy Spirit. This is the most difficult verse because many translations have 'made partakers of the Holy Spirit'. The word translated in the NIV as 'shared' is just as accurately translated 'partakers', but the key to understanding the author is in the verb translated as 'made' or 'become'. In the Greek it is 'becoming', not the past tense 'become'. The difference is extremely important. If a person has become a partaker of the Holy Spirit they are born again, they have not only tasted, but swallowed. But if a person is on the journey towards being born again, we must use 'becoming' because the process, although almost complete, has not been completed.

Every word that the author uses has been carefully chosen to speak of someone that the Lord has brought along a journey of revelation, right up to the point of then commanding them to be born again. But this person has turned away and rejected God's offer. This is why the author writes in the beginning, *it is impossible...if they should fall away to be brought back to repentance.* The word impossible cannot be diluted to mean there is any possibility of coming back to that place of repentance. Why? Because this person has committed a sin which leads to death, the unpardonable sin.

Like the two million Jews who refused to enter the land, this person has sealed their fate. The Lord has done all in His power to make them trust Him for salvation, but He will never force a person to take that step into the river. Only Joshua and Caleb of that generation received what was promised, the rest never entered the Promised Land, for God swore on oath that they would die in the desert. He told Moses He was going to destroy them all, but decided to let them live out their days, however, the oath stood firm (Numbers 14).

It is the Lord who draws the seeker, calls the seeker, reveals Himself to the seeker, gives the seeker a taste, gives the seeker His promises, it is He who does all of this, but if, when he has brought them lovingly all the way to the cross and opened their eyes to all He offers, if they still refuse to trust in Him, what is left for Him to do? He will never force His will on them, but if they can experience all that and walk away, they turn their back on Christ's sacrifice, they spit on the cross and blatantly despise God's free gift, *they are crucifying the Son of God all over again and subjecting him to public disgrace (Hebrews 6:6)*

Therefore, the Lord turns His back on them, He will never bring them back to that place. No person comes to the Lord unless called. In this case, the person has forfeited the opportunity to ever be called again, for there is nothing else to offer them.

This is the situation John is referring to in the verses we are studying, and such is the reason he says *I am not saying he should pray about that.* There is no point in praying for someone who God has rejected, for *it is impossible to renew them to repentance.* In this case they are rejected because they have rejected His offer of salvation, brought the cross to 'disgrace', and walked away.

And finally, notice that John refers his readers back to chapter three with these words in our study passage.

18 *We know that anyone born of God does not continue to sin; the one who was born of God keeps him safe, and the evil one does not touch him.* 19 *We know that we are children of God, and that the whole world is under the control of the evil one.*

As we saw in study ten, the root of sin, which is rebellion against God, has been destroyed in those who are born of God. In this sense they cannot continue to sin, for their ego, the self-ruling principle, is crucified with Christ. The true Christian repents when he commits sins, the non-Christian refuses to repent. Here, John is clarifying his position again. Those who have committed the sin which leads to death are not children of God and never will be, they remain under the control of the evil one.

Summary

Whenever we are dealing with difficult passages of Scripture, as with all Scripture, applying the fundamental principles of exegesis, such as context, are of upmost importance. In this last chapter John is giving his final remarks, he is summing up all he has written, and therefore we must interpret in light of what has gone before. It is very unusual to find any verse in the New Testament where an apostle is suggesting a topic we needn't pray about. It is obvious from the context that John is not speaking of physical death, for the entire message of this letter is to call believers to examine their faith.

The fact that John reminds us of his comments in chapter three tells us that he has in mind a person who is still living in rebellion to the will of God, a person who is continuing to sin, who has never surrendered their will, denied self and taken up their cross. There is a great warning here for those who are seeking God, for it seems there is a sin which leads to eternal spiritual death, a point at which God turns His back.

In Romans 1:24-26, when speaking of those who rejected God, turned to worshipping images, and homosexuality, Paul uses the phrase that 'God gave them over'. This phrase means to 'let them go their own way'. The same is said of Esau whom God 'hated'. This is not an emotional hate, but rather the opposite of love which takes action to save. This word, in this context, means to let someone go without regard because this person has gone too far to be redeemed.

In my opinion this is the sin John is referring to, a form of sin which, after knowing the truth, totally rejects the truth. There is always the possibility of repentance for the ignorant, for the person who has only intellectually rejected Christ. But for those who have been lead by the Lord, understood the grace of God and His promises, experienced the conviction of the Holy Spirit, if such a person can then contemplate the cross of Christ and walk away, there remains nothing more to bring them to repentance.

Study Seventeen

The Twelfth Mark: Overcomers

1st John 5:3-5

3 This is love for God: to obey his commands. And his commands are not burdensome, 4 for everyone born of God overcomes the world. This is the victory that has overcome the world, even our faith. 5 Who is it that overcomes the world? Only he who believes that Jesus is the Son of God.

Introduction

There are a great many professing Christians whose lives are entangled with the world. For such people, double standards, compromise and worldliness are so entrenched into their way of life that it is difficult to believe they have any idea of what John means when he writes of overcoming the world, indeed, he would say that they are not Christians at all!

What does John mean by 'the world?' In 2:16 John uses the following categories: 'the cravings of sinful man, the lust of his eyes and the boasting of what he has and does.' We discussed these issues in study five so need not repeat them in detail here, but John's message is clear. If a person is still in love with what this world has to offer, if they are still driven by and a slave to their fleshly desires, worldly ambitions, and boasting of who they are and their material accomplishments, then such a person is not born of God, they still belong to the world which enslaves them.

John leaves no room for compromise or doubt in this letter. In 2:15 he tells his readers 'not to love the world or anything in the world', meaning the world system of rebellion against God, and then states that 'if anyone loves the world, the love of the Father is not in him.' John's command is both radical and uncompromising. Why? Because he recognizes that those who have experienced new birth came to that experience through the revelation that the world was dragging them into hell and eternal separation from Jesus Christ. How could anyone who has experienced this revelation, and surrendered to the saving arms of Christ, still love that which was the enemy of his soul?

Therefore, in this final chapter of his letter he states categorically that 'everyone born of God overcomes the world'. In this study we will examine John's final mark of a true Christian, and test ourselves as to whether or not we are what he calls 'overcomers'.

Slave or Overcomer?

In order to understand John's teaching we will firstly look at some examples of those who recognized their inability to overcome. The gospels are set within the context of the Old Covenant, and therefore, obviously none of the people who encountered Jesus were born again. Regeneration begins on the Day of Pentecost, for this was when the Holy Spirit first took up residence within those who desired to be free from sin. As we read stories from the gospels we can clearly see the powerlessness of people who are not born again.

Overcoming Unbelief.

In Mark 9: 14-32 we have the account of Jesus casting a demon out of a boy who was possessed by a deaf and dumb spirit. The boy's father had asked Jesus' disciples to cast out the demon and they were unable, even though they had previously received authority to do this and had driven out many demons (Mark 6: 7, 13). After hearing this report from the boy's father, Jesus sounds almost indignant when He calls them an "unbelieving generation", and states "how long shall I stay with you", and "how long shall I put up with you."

The child is brought to Jesus and the father asks, 'if you can do anything, take pity on us and help us'. Jesus' reply is revealing and challenging as He repeats the man's question back to him. " 'If you can? Everything is possible for him who believes." This statement is not only for the boy's father, but also for His disciples. Essentially Jesus is asking 'do you believe I can?' The father immediately replies with a statement that shows both his desire to believe, for the sake of himself and his son, and his battle with unbelief.

"I do believe; help me overcome my unbelief!"

How can a person who is not born of God overcome their unbelief? They cannot! Why? For the simple reason that they have not entrusted their life to Christ, they have not crossed the line of trusting God by faith, they have not experienced the life-changing gift of salvation. Faith is a gift from God, not something we can manufacture through sheer will-power. Faith is kindled in the human heart as the Lord draws people to a place of surrender, that place where hope becomes reality, the faith Peter calls a 'certain' or 'living hope' through the experience of new birth (1st Peter 1:3).

We overcome unbelief through new birth. Jesus' disciples later asked Him why they were unable to cast out the demon and He told them that it could only come out through prayer. But He ended this discussion by telling them that He would be betrayed, killed, and in three days rise again. Jesus pointed to His sacrifice on the cross as the answer to their question. Yes, the demon could only come out with prayer, but, if they were born again they would have known that, because the indwelling Holy Spirit would reveal it to them.

But the Holy Spirit would not come until Christ had died and risen, and only after this would they be born again. From that day onwards, and until the end of their lives, Jesus' disciples would never ask "why could we not cast it out", for they would be men led by the Holy Spirit within them.

Overcoming Fear.

In Luke 8 we have two stories which mention fear. In the first, the disciples are in a boat with Jesus during a raging storm and believe they are all going to drown (Luke 8:22-25). The Lord is sleeping, although I imagine waves are splashing over the sides of the boat and He is completely aware of what is happening. The disciples decide to wake Him up, supposedly to discuss how they were going to save this carpenter and themselves.

Most likely the majority of Jesus' disciples were pretty good swimmers, considering the techniques they used for fishing, but Jesus was the son of a carpenter, a man unaccustomed to working on a dangerous lake. In any case, they were certainly not prepared for what came next. Jesus gets up, rebukes the waves, the storm subsides and He asks them 'where is your faith'.

Mark records that *in fear amazement they asked one another, "Who is this? he commands even the winds and the water, and they obey him."*

In the second story Jesus confronts the legion of demons in the man from Gerasenes, a naked man chained hand and foot, kept under guard, who broke his chains and now lived in a solitary place (Luke 8:26-39). Jesus allowed the demons to enter a herd of pigs which proceeded to charge over a steep bank and into the lake where they drowned. The herdsmen reported the incident and the townspeople came to find this man they had been terrified of, sitting at Jesus' feet, dressed, cured, and in his right mind.

Mark tells us that after seeing the evidence, *'all the people of the region of Gerasenes asked Jesus to leave them, because they were overcome with fear'.*

What do these two stories have in common, and why were both groups, the disciples and people of Gerasenes, so filled with fear? The answer is simple. They were afraid of Jesus because they could not comprehend the incredible power He had. The storm had obeyed Him, the demons had obeyed Him. The disciples, as good Jewish men who believed in one God, were too afraid to speculate about a person who could control nature, and the Gerasenes likely thought He was a god walking on the earth.

In any case, the power that Jesus demonstrated terrified them all, their fear overcame them because they didn't know who He truly was, didn't know that He was there to bring them to salvation.

Yet after the disciples were born of God, only then did they really know the extent of Jesus' mission, and only then did all their fears dissolve. They no longer feared Him, or those who opposed them, nor did they fear death or anything this world could threaten them with, for each of them died as martyrs, men who had overcome the world through the new birth that made them citizens of another kingdom. It is only through truly knowing Christ and experiencing new birth that we can have the courage to overcome fear, for that courage is not our own, but Christ in us.

Overcoming the World

Many professing Christians cannot understand the radical Biblical portrayal of 'the world' because of their circumstances and the land in which they live. If we live in a country where Christianity is respected, tolerated, and even celebrated, the world may seem like a friendly place we are passing through on our journey to a better place. However, if we live in a country where Christians are hated, church buildings are burned to the ground, pastors are beaten or murdered and Christians constantly persecuted, the world is not a friendly place, but enemy territory, a place we must endure, a place our faith is severely tested until the Lord takes us to our real home.

The latter is closest to the Biblical understanding of the world. Although we know with absolute certainty that God is Sovereign, He has allowed this world to be temporarily under the control of Satan and those Scripture calls the 'rulers of this age', demons and principalities who oppose God's plan of salvation vehemently. As Paul explains,

11 Put on the full armor of God so that you can take your stand against the devil's schemes. 12 For our struggle is not against flesh and blood, but against the rulers, against the authorities, against the dark powers of this dark world and against the spiritual forces of evil in the heavenly realms (Ephesians 6:11-12).

Added to this are Paul's comments in Romans 13:1-7 where he tells believers that we must submit to governing authorities as these have been established by God to keep order and administer punishment to wrongdoers. He concludes about paying taxes and revenue, giving respect and honor. During these verses Paul says the following words which I think help us to understand his overall thinking.

Therefore, it is necessary to submit to the authorities, not only because of possible punishment but also because of conscience (Romans 13:5).

Paul recognizes that Christians live in enemy territory and that we are 'citizens of heaven' and 'ambassadors of Christ', two terms he uses in his letters. He also recognizes that governments, in general, are interested in the welfare of the people and the peaceful governing of laws to maintain a stable environment without chaos. It is in this context that he says that God has instituted human authorities, because in such an environment the gospel can be preached.

On the other hand, Paul recognizes that Satan does all he can to raise up ungodly dictators, create chaos, prohibit the gospel, and encourage practices which violate the moral principles of God's Word. All this should make it clear to us that this world is both a physical and spiritual battleground. Paul uses the word 'conscience' in the verse above, a word I consider extremely important in this discussion, for this word draws us to the fact that Christians are to be led by the Holy Spirit in deciding matters of morality, obedience, and even civil disobedience.

Throughout Church history some have tried to create what we call Christendom, the idea of a country being governed by Christian values and Biblical laws. The Roman Catholic Church tried to achieve this end, as did John Calvin in Geneva shortly after the Protestant Reformation. Both failed, and failed miserably, for one simple reason! You cannot change the human heart with regulations and laws; the best you can do is to control it with the threat of punishment.

The Marks of an Overcomer

The result and effect of true regeneration is to overcome the world and all it offers us. Those who are born *of* God are born *for* God. Through faith in Christ Jesus we have been brought into another world, another realm, a different kingdom. We no longer serve the prince of this world (Satan), but rather, we belong to the King of Kings whose kingdom is not of this world (John 18:36).

...4 for everyone born of God overcomes the world. This is the victory that has overcome the world, even our faith. 5 Who is it that overcomes the world? Only he who believes that Jesus is the only Son of God (1st John 5:4-5).

True faith in Christ results in regeneration, results in being in Christ, therefore, what He loves, we love. To be born again is to be made new, a new heart, new desires and new purpose for life. The old man desired the things of this world because he belonged to this world, he chased after worldly things trying to fill the god-shaped void within him. Faith in Christ is the vehicle which brings all this about, and in that faith is the promise of victory. Faith in Christ is our foundational armor in fighting the spiritual battle, for He is our captain.

...In this world you will have trouble. But take heart! I have overcome the world (John 16:33).

The One who has overcome the world leads us through this world. He has provided us with the weapons we need in order to have victory, weapons which are forged in the fire of faith. He has walked through this world, being 'tempted in all things', but He stands victorious over Satan, corrupt authorities, and all this world has to offer. We who are in Him share in His victory. The deeper we are in the love of Christ the more this visible world fades. The cross is our focus, for it is there the world was conquered by our Lord. As we focus on the cross it becomes like a telescope, bringing into sight a glimpse of a far off country, like all those who lived and died by faith, those recorded in Hebrews 11.

13 All these people were still living by faith when they died...and they admitted they were aliens and strangers on the earth. 14 People who say such things show that they are looking for a country of their own. 15 If they were thinking of the country they had left, they would have the opportunity to return. 16 Instead, they were longing for a better country - a heavenly one. Therefore God is not ashamed to be called their God, for he has prepared a city for them (Hebrews 11:14-16).

Summary

John tells us that only he who believes that Jesus is the Son of God overcomes the world. John is not speaking of intellectual belief, but the radical, life-changing faith which is only found in those who have been born from above, those who have surrendered their lives to Christ. Some falsely believe that they can accept Jesus into their lives and still retain control of their lives. Perhaps these were the unfortunate recipients of weak and powerless forms of evangelism, that same form of evangelism that produces weak and powerless converts whose eyes are still closed to the invisible kingdom.

Such people cannot overcome the world because they still belong to the world. One cannot overcome that which he is still in love with, that which still owns his heart. He who is still a child of this world has to die and a new man be born who is not of this world, a spiritual man born into the family of God, a child of heaven.

The call to salvation is a command to reject this world and become a citizen of another world, one we cannot see with worldly eyes. This transformation is a spiritual one and a mysterious thing, an invisible gift which can only be received by surrendering all in faith. One of the proofs that this transformation has occurred is our rejection of the world which enslaved us, a hatred for the base desires, ambitions and lusts which held us captive in our unsaved state. How could we still love the very thing which kept us from freedom, the thing which blinded our eyes to the promises of God?

Christ died to deliver us from the world. He is the overcomer, the only sinless one who took our sins upon Himself so that we could share in His victory through faith in Him. He has gone to prepare a place for us, those of us who are aliens and strangers on this earth, and when we finally leave this worldly place, we will walk into the city of God and know we are home.

Also by Steve Copland

Colossians

Living in Christ: Bible Study/Commentary series.

The Apostle Paul's letter to the Colossians contains some of the most profound statements ever written about the Lord Jesus Christ and status of believers. The heresy of Gnosticism had taken root and was spreading throughout the fledgling Gentile churches, a heresy which spearheaded Satan's attack on Christianity for over a hundred years.

Gnosticism challenged the fundamental doctrines of the Divinity and humanity of Christ, split the Church into levels of spirituality, promoted ecstatic experiences and the worship of angels, asceticism and the keeping of rules and traditions.

This series of twenty studies explores and applies Paul's inspired answers to all of these topics, challenges the resurgent Gnostic heresies which have resurrected in the past thirty years, and encourages Christians to know their true status in Christ.

1st Peter.

Living in Christ: Bible Study/Commentary Series

Every Christian faces storms in life. Throughout the world many are being persecuted, even murdered for their faith. And there are other forms of suffering which may not threaten our lives; physical pain, emotional

174

pain, broken dreams, conflicts, tensions and stress. Peter's message, written under the inspiration of the Holy Spirit, offers good news to Christians.

God has given us the power and strength to face any and every situation, power to overcome every form of suffering, and the peace and calm which is always present in those who know Jesus Christ as Lord.

This first letter of Peter's is filled with encouragement in the face of suffering, instructions on how we must live as God's holy people, advise on our attitudes towards government and secular authorities, and teaching for husbands, wives, and elders. Peter also calls us to be prepared to speak to those who ask us about our faith in Christ, and instructs us on how to reply.

Mary Magdalene: A Woman Who Loved

1st Century Trilogy - Book One

Throughout history there has been much written about Mary of Magdala, most of it legend and speculation, some of it derogatory. The Bible, however, gives us many clues as to the character, personality and contributions this first century woman made to the ministry of Christ and the early church. This book is, in many ways, a tribute to a woman whose life was dramatically changed by the one she came to love more than life itself.

Mary Magdalene was a woman whose life circumstances led her from demonic possession and prostitution to being the first witness of the greatest event in world history. In an attempt to reconstruct her life, this book demonstrates her struggle as she confronts the patriarchal traditions embedded in first century culture, the hypocritical practice of condemning only one gender in adultery, her transformation as she finds grace, freedom and real love in her encounter with Christ, and her being chosen as 'the apostle to the apostles'.

This novel takes the reader into the first century. It delves into the personal lives of lepers, cripples and the sight impaired; it goes on a journey from the battlefields of ancient Germania to Jerusalem with two Roman soldiers who end up initiated into the cult of Mithraism; it explores the fears, prejudices and arrogance of the religious rulers of Israel, and the ambitions of Judas Iscariot; it portrays the everyday struggles of first century people in an occupied land; it looks behind the scenes at a woman who is seduced into committing adultery and used to test Jesus, and brings them all together beneath the cross of Jesus Christ.

Simon and Simon: Passion and Power

1st Century Trilogy - Book Two

Simon and Simon is the second novel of the 1st century trilogy. It features two men born just a few miles apart whose lives are dramatically different, Simon Peter and Simon Magus. Simon Peter's life weaves through the story and is contrasted with Magus, the one known as 'Simon the Sorcerer'. The latter travels to Kashmir and studies the Rig Veda in search of individual power. He returns to Israel where he meets Simon Peter. Both end up in Rome: one levitates for Nero, the other is crucified. Triarius is a Roman soldier married for only a few months and sent to the Northern frontier. His wife is pregnant when he leaves and believed to be carrying a son, if the witch was correct. He sends orders to dispose of the child if the hag is mistaken. His wife gives birth to a daughter, 'Triaria', and secretly raises the child while her husband is away, not knowing if he will return. He does, and discovers the child's existence, and…well that would be telling the story.

Religion: History and Mystery

War, Power, Greed, Jihad, Inquisition, Crusades and Extremists, all words we associate with religion. Shamans, priests, prophets and magicians, servants of the gods, mediums of power, or frauds? 22 religions, examined, exposed and deciphered.

Religion: History and Mystery explores the ancient and modern religions which have dominated the world for 6000 years, exposes the contradictions, uncovers the mysteries, and reveals the truth of who and what we are. This book also points out why Judaism and Christianity are so incredibly distinct from every other religion. Is there a Divine Mystery contained in the Bible which is absent in all other religious texts?

Running the Race

Every generation of Christians face challenges in 'running the race of faith'. Living for Christ in the 21st Century is no exception. The Apostle Paul warned that 'the time will come when men will not put up with sound doctrine. Instead, to suit their own desires, they will gather around them a great number of teachers to say what their itching ears want to hear'. We are living in such times.

We should not be surprised, for Jesus warned us there would be many false prophets in the Last Days before His return. 'Running the Race' challenges the extremes, throws light on the shadows, and illuminates the path which Christ has set before those who have trusted Him with their lives.

Slug: The Reluctant Butterfly

Slug wants to fly, but he doesn't want to die. Slug is a beautiful story about our reluctance to allow God to transform us into what He wants us to become. Slug learns through his mistakes that many will lead us down wrong paths, but obedience to our Creator brings complete joy and fulfillment. Grunt, a crow and central character in the story, discovers the pitfalls of peer pressure, the power of forgiveness, and eventual self acceptance in his new life. (Children ages 7-11)

Time for Truth: A Challenge to Skeptics

Time for truth challenges skeptics to take a fresh look at the supernatural qualities of the Bible. Issues such as the existence of God, creation/evolution, evil and suffering are discussed, and the reader is taken on a logical, scientific and inspiring walk through world history as a story of God's plan for humanity.

This book has been used in various forms since 1985 when it was first written for a man dying of cancer. He refused to speak of God. He was an ardent atheist;

however, he had a spiritual transformation just three days before he died and witnessed of his faith in Christ.

Perfection

Within the human soul a voice calls us to reach for perfection. In every area of our lives we demonstrate a desire to know, experience and create that which is perfect. The clothes we wear, the flowers we choose, religions we practice and love we seek, all testify to our instinct to reject that which we perceive as flawed, and strive for beauty, contentment and fulfillment. Is it possible for us to know and experience perfection? The answer is 'yes'.

Just Because: The Story of Salvation for Children

Just Because takes children on an exciting and inspirational journey through the Bible. It gives them an exciting bird's-eye-view of God's plan unfolding as He prepares the world for the coming of Jesus Christ. Throughout the story Satan is watching out for the child who will "crush his head," (Genesis 3) and he endeavors to stop God's plan from unfolding.

The reader knows who that special child is, and the story especially opens up the insights that point to Jesus throughout the Old Testament. Each Study takes about twenty minutes to read and ends with a short Biblical lesson. Children love it.

The King's Donkeys

Donkey lived a long time ago in a town called Nazareth. His master was a carpenter who married Mary, the young woman who gave birth to the Son of God. He was there when Jesus was born, saw the shepherds and wise men, travelled to Egypt, watched Jesus grow up, and became the donkey of the King of Kings.

This children's book, a work of fiction, tells the story of Jesus through the eyes of a donkey. The book contains 22 original paintings and is for children 5 years and over.

Contact details for conference, seminar and book enquiries.

www.stevecopland.com
copland56@yahoo.co.nz
Facebook: Steve Copland

Made in the USA
Coppell, TX
03 November 2020